W9-BKG-556

EXILIC
PREACHING

EXILIC PREACHING

Testimony for Christian Exiles in an Increasingly Hostile Culture

Edited by Erskine Clarke

TRINITY PRESS INTERNATIONAL
Harrisburg, Pennsylvania

Unless otherwise indicated, biblical quotations are from the New Revised Standard Version, copyright 1989 by The Division of Christian Education of the National Council of the Churches of Christ in the United States of America.

Excerpt from "East Coker" in *Four Quartets,* copyright 1943 by T. S. Eliot and renewed 1971 by Esme Valerie Eliot, reprinted by permission of Harcourt Brace & Company.

Excerpt from "A Letter to John Donne" in *Collected Poems 1998 Edition,* copyright 1998 by C. H. Sisson, reprinted by permission of Carcanet Press Limited.

Copyright © 1998 by Trinity Press International

All rights reserved. No part of this book may be reproduced, stored in a retrieval system, or transmitted, in any form or by any means, electronic, mechanical, photocopying, recording, or otherwise, without the written permission of the publisher.

Trinity Press International, P.O. Box 1321, Harrisburg, PA 17105
Trinity Press International is a division of the Morehouse Group

Library of Congress Cataloging-in-Publication Data
Exilic preaching : testimony for Christian exiles in an increasingly
   hostile culture / edited by Erskine Clarke.
      p.   cm.
   Includes bibliographical references.
   ISBN 1-56338-246-6 (pbk. : alk. paper)
   1. Preaching – United States. I. Clarke, Erskine, 1941- .
BV4211.2.E95   1998
251'.00973 – dc21   98-41028

Printed in the United States of America

98   99   00   01   02   10   9   8   7   6   5   4   3   2   1

Contents

ACKNOWLEDGMENTS

Chapters in this book first appeared in the following issues of *Journal for Preachers:*

WALTER BRUEGGEMANN

1. "Preaching to Exiles," Pentecost 1993 (XVI–4)
2. "Cadences Which Redescribe: Speech among Exiles," Easter 1994 (XVII–3)
3. "Duty as Delight and Desire: Preaching Obedience That Is Not Legalism," Advent 1994 (XVII–1)

STANLEY M. HAUERWAS

4. "Practice Preaching," Advent 1994 (XVII–1)
5. "Embodied Memory," Easter 1996 (XIX–3)
6. "Hating Mothers as the Way to Peace," Pentecost 1988 (XI–4)

BARBARA BROWN TAYLOR

7. "Preaching the Terrors," Lent 1992 (XV–2)
8. "Preaching into the Next Millennium," Easter 1996 (XIX–3)
9. "The Easter Sermon," Easter 1995 (XVIII–3)

WILLIAM H. WILLIMON

10. "Postmodern Preaching: Learning to Love the Thickness of the Text," Easter 1996 (XIX–3)
11. "Preaching in an Age That Has Lost Its Moral Compass," Easter 1995 (XVIII–3)
12. "Easter Preaching as Peculiar Speech," Easter 1994 (XVII–3)

Reprinted with permission of *Journal for Preachers,*
P.O. Box 520, Decatur, GA 30031-0520.

INTRODUCTION

During the closing decades of the twentieth century, a growing number of commentators have reported on the crisis of the church in North America. Robert Wuthnow, for example, has analyzed *The Restructuring of American Religion;*[1] Dean Hoge, Benton Johnson, and Donald Luidens have chronicled *Vanishing Boundaries: The Religion of Mainline Protestant Baby Boomers;*[2] and Nicholas Lash has told of *The Beginning and End of "Religion."*[3] This book is about preaching in the midst of the crisis.

For many, the crisis is most clearly visible in the disappearance of the "social function the churches once fulfilled in American life"[4] and in the domestication of the churches revealed in this social dislocation. Churches no longer provide legitimization or support to social and moral order. Mainline Protestant denominations, once the proud bearers of cultural power and authority, have seen their numbers and influence slide steadily away from the center toward the margins of American social and culture life. The Roman Catholic Church has lost much of its social function in the older ethnic enclaves and, while moving toward a more central place in American society, has been unable to occupy successfully the cultural ground lost by the Protestant mainstream. Evangelical and Pentecostal churches have emerged from the marginalization they experienced earlier in the twentieth century, but in spite of vigorous efforts by some to create a "moral major-

---

1. Robert Wuthnow, *The Restructuring of American Religion: Society and Faith since World War II* (Princeton, N.J.: Princeton University Press, 1988).
2. Dean Hoge, R. Benton Johnson, and Donald Luidens, *Vanishing Boundaries: The Religion of Mainline Protestant Baby Boomers* (Louisville: Westminster/John Knox, 1994).
3. Nicholas Lash, *The Beginning and End of "Religion"* (Cambridge: Cambridge University Press, 1996).
4. George R. Hunsberger and Craig Van Gelder, eds., *The Church between Gospel and Culture: The Emerging Mission in North America* (Grand Rapids: Eerdmans, 1996), xiii. For important examples of the literature on the church's crisis, see also Jackson W. Carroll and Wade Clark Roof, eds., *Beyond Establishment: Protestant Identity in a Post-Protestant Age* (Louisville: Westminster/John Knox, 1996); Wade Clark Roof and William McKinney, eds., *Reimagining Denominationalism* (New York: Oxford University Press, 1994); and William Placher, *The Domestication of Transcendence: How Modern Thinking about God Went Wrong* (Louisville: Westminster/John Knox, 1996).

ity" or a culturally dominant "Christian coalition," they remain largely frustrated in their hopes of a "Christian America."

Beneath these many signs of a shift in the social functions of the churches lie the great transformations of Western society that have marked the twentieth century and that have been gathered together under the rubrics of *modernity* and *postmodernity*. The task of preaching in the late twentieth century requires that some attention be given to the character of these transformations and their impact on the life of the church in North America.

Modernity, as a social order, promotes large and complex systems. The specialization and efficiency of a technological society, the elevation of means over ends, and the development of a management style suitable for factories and large bureaucracies characterize modernity.[5] Modern styles of organization have deeply penetrated the churches not only at the denominational level but also in the work of ministry as pastors have increasingly become administrators who manage by objective, complex programs.

As a cultural system, modernity has insisted on a division of life into public and private sectors and has drawn a sharp line between the world of facts (which is public) and the world of values (which is private).[6] Such a division, rooted in Enlightenment rationality, has been closely tied to an individualism that promotes an understanding of the self as autonomous and to a culture of consumption. Christianity has been largely privatized within this cultural system, and faith has been made primarily a matter of personal piety. The churches have been left as voluntary associations to nurture such piety.

Since the 1960s emerging new social and cultural realities have been named *postmodern* as they appear to many observers to be replacing the dominant systems of modernity. While no definition of postmodernism has conquered the field of competing interpretations, certain broad characteristics have been widely acknowledged. A growing pluralism is said to have largely shaped the social character of postmodernism. This pluralism is not only the reality of multiple voices speaking at the same time in their own languages out of a

---

5. The most thorough critique of modernity remains Jacques Ellul's *The Technological Society* (New York: Vintage, 1964).

6. See Michael Polanyi, *Personal Knowledge: Towards a Post-Critical Philosophy* (Chicago: University of Chicago Press, 1958).

myriad of social and cultural contexts; it is also an honoring of this diversity. Pluralism, in a postmodern world, is good. The domination and control of the social order by one group — mainline or evangelical Protestants, for example — is bad.

On the cultural level, postmodernism denies the existence of any single system of objective truth. All truth is private truth.[7] Any attempt, it is said, to claim a center, an essence, or an essential purpose to human life is a political act.[8] Moreover, we create in our own minds the world in which we live. Consequently, among the results of postmodernism is a narcissistic culture preoccupied with self and with a therapeutic quest for "self-fulfillment."[9] The domestication of the church within such a culture speaks of an even deeper level of crisis than the loss of the church's traditional social function within U.S. society. A comfortably domesticated church has abandoned theological language, and the way of understanding the world that the language represents, for the language and world of therapy. "Unhealthy" and "healthy," for example, have largely replaced "sinful" and "righteous."[10]

In the midst of these social and cultural developments of the twentieth century, a new and deeply challenging possibility began to slowly work its way into the consciousness of some North American Christians. It had been assumed that the United States was a place fundamentally hospitable to the Christian faith and that a deep coherence exists between a dominant national cultural and Christian faith and life. To be sure, the inroads of secularity were all too clear — the ways in which a religious worldview and ethos had been eroded by the assumptions and values of the modern world. But the ideology of secularity had insisted on its own neutrality in regard to matters of faith. Within a modern secular society, it was said, space is available for Christian faith, even if that space is personal and not public. In a similar manner, in a postmodern culture with its emphasis on

---

7. See David Harvey, *The Condition of Post-Modernity: An Inquiry into the Origins of Culture Change* (Cambridge: Basil Blackwell, 1984).

8. See especially Michel Foucault's historical studies into madness, punishment, and human sexuality.

9. The classic studies of this therapeutic culture and narcissism remain Philip Rieff, *The Triumph of the Therapeutic: Uses of Faith after Freud*, new ed. (Chicago: University of Chicago Press, 1987); and Christopher Lasch, *The Culture of Narcissism: American Life in an Age of Diminishing Expectations* (New York: Norton, 1978).

10. Robert Bellah et al., *Habits of the Heart: Individualism and Commitment in American Life* (Berkeley: University of California Press, 1985).

diversity, space appeared available to Christian faith and life as one among many faiths and lifestyles. Moreover, the treasured links between Christian communities and U.S. culture appeared to be worthy of continued nurture, especially in regard to common commitments to democracy and civic responsibility.

What began, however, to appear as a possibility as the century moved toward its conclusion was that a voracious consumer society lies beneath both a modern secular culture and a postmodern culture. This society, which feeds on the consumption of goods and good times and which protects itself with a massive military, is not hospitable, or even neutral, but increasingly hostile to Christian faith and life. Evidences of the hostility have long appeared in "high culture" and more recently and powerfully in the "popular culture" of television and the entertainment and advertising industries. Pagan gods, long thought conquered by Christianity and Western rationality, have come boldly out of hiding to make their ancient claims for sex, violence, and prosperity as the gods worthy to be worshiped. Once again the church is being called upon to confront their power and wrath and their profound hostility to Christian faith and life.[11]

As the churches have sought to explore both the challenges and opportunities of this present crisis, three metaphors have emerged that promise guidance for the way forward. The first metaphor, closely associated with the work of Leslie Newbigin, speaks of Western civilization as "a mission field." In a series of important books, Newbigin called for the "missionary encounter of the gospel with our Western culture."[12] Newbigin was particularly concerned with the ways in which a "modern scientific worldview" dominates Western culture and has created a dichotomy between "facts" — discovered by the methods of science according to laws of cause and effect — and values, the private opinions of individuals. Returning to Britain after years as a missionary in India, Newbigin was struck by how deeply the churches had entered into and adopted the "plausibility structure" of a modern scientific worldview. The consequence of such accommodation was

---

11. Cf. W. A. Visser't Hooft, "Evangelism in the Neo-Pagan Situation," *International Review of Mission* 63, no. 49 (January 1974): 81–86.

12. See especially, Leslie Newbigin, *The Other Side of 1984: Questions for the Churches* (Geneva: WCC Publications, 1984); *Foolishness to the Greeks: The Gospel and Western Culture* (Grand Rapids: Eerdmans, 1986); and *The Gospel in a Pluralist Society* (Grand Rapids: Eerdmans, 1989).

the loss of the gospel's claim to be about the meaning and purpose of human history. Newbigin's call for a "missionary encounter of the gospel with our Western culture" was also a call for the church to enter deeply once again into the "plausibility structure" of the Bible in order to proclaim that the gospel is true and true for all.

A second metaphor is that of "resident aliens," as proposed by Stanley Hauerwas and William Willimon in their widely discussed *Resident Aliens: Life in the Christian Colony*. They aim in the book to challenge the lingering assumptions that the United States is a Christian nation, a hospitable home for the church, and to "show what a marvelous opportunity awaits those pastors and laity who sense what an adventure it is to be the church, people who reside here and now, but who live here as aliens, people who know that, while we live here, 'our commonwealth is in heaven.'"[13] A church of resident aliens presents the world with an "alternative *polis*, a countercultural social structure called the church. It seeks to influence the world by being the church, that is, by being something the world is not and can never be, lacking the gift of faith and vision, which is ours in Christ."[14]

A third metaphor, that of exile, is suggested in the work of Hauerwas and Willimon and more fully developed in the Old Testament studies of Walter Brueggemann.[15] This metaphor provides a way to acknowledge the sense of loss and homelessness that comes with displacement and the opportunities such a displacement provides for recovering a core identity. *Exile*, as a metaphor for the church in North America at the end of the twentieth century, suggests the tasks for all those called to preach the gospel in this unsettled time and provides the theme of *Exilic Preaching*. The essays and sermons of this book were first published in the *Journal for Preachers*.[16] The journal, which was begun in the 1970s by a group of ministers, has been concerned with the task of preaching the gospel in an increasingly hostile environment. Because, however, the environment has not al-

---

13. Stanley M. Hauerwas and William H. Willimon, *Resident Aliens: Life in the Christian Colony* (Nashville: Abingdon, 1989), 29.

14. Ibid., 46.

15. See especially Walter Brueggemann, "Disciplines of Readiness," in *Occasional Paper No. 1*, Theology and Worship Unit, Presbyterian Church (U.S.A.), Louisville, 1989; "Rethinking Church Models through Scripture," *Theology Today* 48 (July 1991): 128–38; *The Threat of Life: Sermons on Pain, Power, and Weakness* (Minneapolis: Fortress, 1996); and *Theology of the Old Testament: Testimony, Dispute, Advocacy* (Minneapolis: Fortress, 1997).

16. *Journal for Preachers*, Columbia Theological Seminary, Box 520, Decatur, GA 30030.

ways looked hostile, but often like a well-loved home, the task of faithful preaching has not appeared simple but complex, evoking not only different interpretations of what is faithful but also conflicts of the heart. Such conflicts are perhaps a part of moving away from a familiar home or of discovering that what we had thought was home had no welcome mat for us. But such a move and such a discovery provide new opportunities for freedom and faithfulness. The essays and sermons that follow point the way toward that freedom and faithfulness.

Two essays by Walter Brueggemann address directly the issue of exilic preaching: "Cadences Which Redescribe: Speech among Exiles" and "Preaching to Exiles." Brueggemann's third essay proposes "Duty as Delight and Desire." To suggest in our preaching, in the midst of our narcissistic and therapeutic culture, that duty might be a delight and desire is an astonishing countercultural proposal, a proposal well suited for exiles struggling with issues of identity and faithfulness.

In one essay, Stanley Hauerwas explores the "practice of preaching" as the activity of a whole community. Such a practice, which is by and for the church, helps exiles "locate our lives in God's story." Two sermons by Hauerwas, "Embodied Memory" and "Hating Mothers as the Way to Peace," illustrate how extraordinarily odd exilic preaching can sound — especially to ears accustomed to hearing culturally relevant sermons.

Barbara Brown Taylor offers three essays on the task of preaching to exiles. While she does not directly utilize the exile metaphor, her articles reflect a profound awareness of the exilic character of the church in late-twentieth-century North America. In "Preaching the Terrors" she draws the reader deep into Lenten themes, and in the "Easter Sermon" she invites the preacher to ponder mysteries beyond our control. Her essay "Preaching into the Next Millennium" addresses "the great shift going on all around us" and calls for not only changes in our preaching but changes in us.

Will Willimon, as might be expected from his writings, forcefully turns his attention to the preacher and to the conversion required of those of us who preach. For Willimon, exilic preaching needs preachers who believe that the gospel is true and who lead lives that reflect such a belief. In "Postmodern Preaching: Learning to Love the Thickness of the Text," he contrasts preaching that operates out of old, familiar plausibility structures with preaching that is speech among exiles. In "Preaching in an Age That Has Lost Its Moral Compass," Willimon addresses not the corruptions of the culture but the moral confusion of the clergy and links that confusion to our preaching: "We would be better people, you and I, if we were more faithful preachers. Clergy ethics has its basis in homiletics." In his article "Easter Preaching as Peculiar Speech," Willimon insists that "our preaching ought to be so confrontative, so in violation of all that contemporary Americans think they know, that it requires no less than a miracle to be heard."

Each of these articles standing alone invites careful reconsideration of our preaching in the midst of the crisis of the church today. Taken together, the articles are a powerful summons to a new exilic preaching. "Exile," writes Brueggemann, "did not lead Jews in the Old Testament to abandon faith or to settle for abdicating despair, nor to retreat to privatistic religion. On the contrary, exile evoked the most brilliant literature and the most daring theological articulation in the Old Testament. There is indeed something characteristically and deeply Jewish about such a buoyant response to trouble, a response that in Christian parlance can only be termed *evangelical*, that is, grounded in a sense and sureness of *news* about God that circumstance cannot undermine or negate." May it be so for us as well.

1

PREACHING TO EXILES

WALTER BRUEGGEMANN

I have elsewhere proposed that the Old Testament experience of and reflection upon exile is a helpful *metaphor* for understanding our current faith situation in the U.S. church and a *model* for pondering new forms of ecclesiology.[1] (Jack Stotts in parallel fashion has suggested that the "period of the Judges" might be a more useful metaphor.[2] Stotts's suggestion has considerable merit, but because we are speaking of metaphors, these suggestions are not mutually exclusive.) The usefulness of a metaphor for rereading our own context is that it is not claimed to be a one-on-one match to "reality," as though the metaphor of "exile" actually *describes* our situation. Rather a metaphor proceeds by having only an odd, playful, and ill-fitting match to its reality, the purpose of which is to illuminate and evoke dimensions of reality that will otherwise go unnoticed and therefore unexperienced.[3]

I

Utilization of the metaphor of exile for the situation of the church in the United States is not easy or obvious, and for some not com-

---

1. My title is reminiscent of E. W. Nicholson's *Preaching to the Exiles: A Study of the Prose Tradition in the Book of Jeremiah* (Oxford: Blackwell, 1970). Nicholson was one of the first in the recent discussion to discern the important role of exile in the generation of Old Testament faith. Nicholson in fact deals only with the late texts in the Book of Jeremiah, which in my discussion I will not take up. Walter Brueggemann, "Disciplines of Readiness," in *Occasional Paper No. 1*, Theology and Worship Unit, Presbyterian Church (U.S.A.), Louisville, 1989; and "Rethinking Church Models through Scripture," *Theology Today* 48 (July 1991): 128–38.

2. Jack Stotts, "Beyond Beginnings," in *Occasional Paper No. 2*, Theology and Worship Unit, Presbyterian Church (U.S.A.), Louisville.

3. On the significance of metaphor for reading the biblical text and for theological reflections, see Phyllis Trible, *God and the Rhetoric of Sexuality*, Overtures to Biblical Theology (Philadelphia: Fortress, 1978), 31–59; and Sallie McFague, *Metaphorical Theology: Models of God in Religious Language* (Philadelphia: Fortress, 1982), 1–66 and passim.

pelling. I suggest the metaphor is more difficult in the South, where establishment Christianity may still be perceived as "alive and well." For those who perceive it so, what follows likely will not be useful or persuasive. My conviction, however, is that even midst such a positive perception of old religious-cultural realities, there is indeed a growing uneasiness about the sustenance of old patterns of faith and life. That uneasiness may be signaled by anxiety about "church growth" and about increasingly problematic denominational budgets.[4]

I wish, however, to tilt the metaphor of exile in a very different direction, one not occupied with issues of institutional well-being or quantitative measure but with the experienced anxiety of "deported" people. That is, my concern is not institutional but pastoral. The exiled Jews of the Old Testament were of course geographically displaced. More than that, however, the exiles experienced a loss of the structured, reliable world that gave them meaning and coherence, and they found themselves in a context where their most treasured and trusted symbols of faith were mocked, trivialized, or dismissed.[5] That is, exile is not primarily geographical, but it is social, moral, and cultural.[6]

Now I believe that this sense of (a) loss of a structured, reliable "world," where (b) treasured symbols of meaning are mocked and dismissed, is a pertinent point of contact between those ancient texts and our situation.[7] On the one hand, I suggest an *evangelical dimension* to exile in our social context. That is, serious, reflective Christians find themselves increasingly at odds with the dominant values of consumer

---

4. In my discussion of the church in relation to pluralism, I have decided not to address what I consider to be the related issue of the faltering of denominations. On that crisis, see Dorothy Bass, "Reflections on the Reports of Decline in Mainstream Protestantism," *Chicago Theological Seminary Register* 79 (1989): 5–15; "Teaching with Authority? The Changing Place of Mainstream Protestantism in American Culture," *Religious Education* 85 (spring 1990): 295–310.

5. On the trivializing of such symbols in the life of ancient Israel, see Peter Ackroyd, "The Temple Vessels: A Continuity Theme," *Vetus Testamentum* 23 (1972): 166–81.

6. Jacob Neusner, *Understanding Seeking Faith: Essays on the Case of Judaism* (Atlanta: Scholars, 1986), 137–41, has shown how the historical-geographical experience of exile has become a paradigm for Judaism, so Jews who did not share the actual concrete experience of exile must nonetheless appropriate its paradigmatic power in order to be fully Jewish. In what follows, I am especially informed by the splendid study of Daniel L. Smith, *The Religion of the Landless: The Social Context of the Babylonian Exile* (Bloomington, Ind.: Meyer Stone, 1989).

7. I use "world" here in the sense of Alfred Schutz, *Phenomenology of the Social World* (Evanston, Ill.: Northwestern University Press, 1967). A more accessible rendering of the same notion of world is found in Peter L. Berger and Thomas Luckmann, *The Social Construction of Reality: A Treatise in the Sociology of Knowledge* (Garden City, N.Y.: Doubleday, 1966).

capitalism and its supportive military patriotism; there is no easy or obvious way to hold together core faith claims and the social realities around us. Reflective Christians are increasingly "resident aliens" (even if one does not accept all of the ethical, ecclesiological extrapolations of Stanley Hauerwas and William Willimon).[8] And if it be insisted that church members are still in places of social power and influence, I suggest that such Christians only need to act and speak out of any serious conviction concerning the public claims of the gospel, and it becomes promptly evident that we are outsiders to the flow of power. I propose that pastors and parishioners together may usefully take into account this changed social reality of the marginalization of faith, a marginalization perhaps felt most strongly by young people.[9]

On the other hand, I suggest a *cultural dimension* to exile that is more "American" than Christian but no less germane to the pastoral task. The "homeland" in which all of us have grown up has been defined and dominated by white, male, Western assumptions that were, at the same time, imposed and also willingly embraced. Exile comes as those values and modes of authority are being effectively and progressively diminished. That diminishment is a source of deep displacement for many, even though for others who are not male and white, it is a moment of emancipation. The deepness of the displacement is indicated, I imagine, by the reactive assault on so-called political correctness, by ugly humor, and by demonizing new modes of power.[10] All these quite visible resistances to the new notwithstanding, we are now required to live in a new situation that for many feels like less than "home." In such a context, folk need pastoral help in relinquishing a home that is gone and in entering a new "dangerous" place that we sense as deeply alien.

I suggest that the exile (as a metaphor) is a rich resource for fresh discernment, even though a *Christian exile* in a secular culture and a *cultural exile* with the loss of conventional hegemony are very

8. Stanley M. Hauerwas and William H. Willimon, *Resident Aliens: Life in the Christian Colony* (Nashville: Abingdon, 1989).

9. The long-term threat to the viability of faith is not right-wing religion, ominous and destructive as that is, but secularism. I think it most unfortunate that the church uses as much energy as it does on the former when the latter is so pervasive and relentless among us.

10. On the theme of "political correctness," see Rosa Ehrenreich, "What Campus Radicals? The P.C. Undergrad Is a Useful Specter," *Harper's*, December 1991, 57–61; and Louis Menand, "What Are Universities For? The Real Crisis on Campus Is One of Identity," *Harper's*, December 1991, 47–56.

different. In fact, the two exiles (evangelical and "American") arise from the fact that establishment Christianity and establishment culture have been in a close, and no longer sustainable, alliance. This quite concrete double focus on exile is a practical manifestation of what Martin Buber has called "an epoch of homelessness," brought on by the intellectual revolution around the figures of Locke, Hobbes, and Descartes, wherein old certitudes have been lost.[11] My interest is, not in a long-term philosophical question, but in the quite specific experience of the present church. I believe that this deep sense of displacement touches us all — liberal and conservative — in personal and public ways. For that reason, the preacher must take into account the place where the faithful church must now live.

II

I propose that in our preaching and more general practice of ministry, we ponder the interface of our *circumstance of exile* (to the extent that this is an appropriate metaphor) and *scriptural resources* that grew from and address the faith crisis of exile. (Note well that this suggested interface entails refocusing our attention, energy, and self-perception. In times when the church could assume its own "establishment," it may have been proper to use prophetic texts to address "kings." But a new circumstance suggests a very different posture for preaching and pastoral authority, now as an exile addressing exiles, in which displacement, failed hopes, anger, wistful sadness, and helplessness permeate our sense of self, sense of community, and sense of future.)

The most remarkable observation one can make about this interface of *exilic circumstance* and *scriptural resources* is this: exile did not lead Jews in the Old Testament to abandon faith or to settle for abdicating despair, nor to retreat to privatistic religion. On the contrary, exile evoked the most brilliant literature and the most daring theological articulation in the Old Testament. There is indeed something characteristically and deeply Jewish about such a buoyant response to trouble,

---

11. Martin Buber, *Between Man and Man* (New York: Macmillan, 1965), 126, writes: "In the history of the human spirit, I distinguish between epochs of habitation and epochs of homelessness." Buber understands our own epoch to be one of homelessness. On the same theme, informed by Buber, see Nicholas Lash, "Eclipse of Word and Presence," *Easter in Ordinary: Reflections on Human Experience and the Knowledge of God* (Charlottesville: University Press of Virginia, 1988), 199–218.

a response that in Christian parlance can only be termed *evangelical*, that is, grounded in a sense and sureness of *news* about God that circumstance cannot undermine or negate. The "news" that generates buoyant theological imagination in ancient Israel is so "hard-core" that it is prerational and does not submit to the "data" of historical circumstance. I suggest this is a time for us when preachers are "liberated" to assert that hard-core, prerational buoyance in a church too much in the grip of the defeatist sensibility of our evident cultural collapse.

For many preachers, this will require considerations of texts (i.e., families of texts) that were not studied in seminary. They were not studied in seminary precisely because exile seemed remote from us, something at the most that belonged to "late Judaism."[12] As a guide into these "new" texts, I suggest three useful resources: (*a*) Peter Ackroyd's *Exile and Restoration* is the classic English text on the subject, providing the "meat and potatoes" of historical criticism;[13] (*b*) Ralph W. Klein's *Israel in Exile*, a more accessible book, exhibits theological, pastoral sensitivity;[14] and (*c*) Daniel Smith's *The Religion of the Landless*, a daring sociohistorical study, is most suggestive for seeing into the visceral elements of the circumstance, literature, and faith of the ancient exiles.[15]

III

While the subject of faith in exile is exceedingly rich, here I suggest six interfaces of the *circumstance of exile* and *scriptural resources:*[16]

1. Exiles must grieve their loss and express their resentful sadness

---

12. The disregard of "late Judaism" in Christian scholarship and theological education reflects the power of the "Wellhausian hypothesis" in which the postexilic period was regarded as degenerate, inferior, and not worthy of attention. More recent scholarship has to some modest extent broken loose of the grip of that hypothesis in order that the period can be taken with theological seriousness.

13. Peter Ackroyd, *Exile and Restoration: A Study of Hebrew Thought of the Sixth Century B.C.*, Old Testament Library (Philadelphia: Westminster, 1968).

14. Ralph W. Klein, *Israel in Exile: A Theological Interpretation*, Overtures to Biblical Theology (Philadelphia: Fortress, 1979).

15. Smith, *The Religion of the Landless*. Smith's study represents a most important advance beyond Ackroyd and Klein in terms of method, as he pays attention to the interaction between the social realities of the exile and its impact upon the way in which literature functions.

16. It is evident that I will proceed with something like a "method of correlation" not unlike that proposed by Paul Tillich. I find such an approach practically useful in establishing a "dynamic analogy" with the text for our own time. The method is a convenience for me and reflects no commitment to a program like that of Tillich, about which I have great reservations.

about what was and now is not and will never again be. In our culture, we must be honest about the waning of our "great days" of world domination (before the rise of the Japanese economy) and all of the awkward economic complications that we experience in quite personal and immediate ways. In the church, we must be honest about the loss of our "great days" when our churches and their pastors, and even our denominations, were forces for reckoning as they are not now. I suggest that congregations must be, in intentional ways, *communities of honest sadness*, naming the losses. We might be Jews on the Ninth of Av, when every year Jews celebrate and grieve the destruction of Jerusalem and its temple complex, in 587 B.C.E., a destruction that persists for Jews in paradigmatic ways.[17] This community of sadness has as its work the countering of the "culture of denial," which continues to imagine that it is as it was, even when our experience tells otherwise.

The obvious place for scriptural resources for such work is in the Book of Lamentations, the text used by Jews for that holy day of grieving on the Ninth of Av. Because the text is "canon," it intends to be used for many sadnesses of a communal kind, well beyond the concrete loss of Jerusalem. In the Book of Lamentations, I suggest three motifs among many that warrant attention: (*a*) the collection of poems begins with a sustained and terrible negativity: "no resting place" (1:3), "no pasture" (1:6), "no one to help" (1:7), "none to comfort" (1:9, 16, 17, 21; 2:13), "no rest" (2:18). The poem is candid and preoccupied about loss. (*b*) The poetic collection ends with a pathos-filled statement (which may be a dependent clause, as in NRSV, or a question, as in RSV). In either case, the final statement is preceded in 5:20 with a haunting question to which Israel does not know the answer, a question about being "forgotten" and "forsaken" by God. (*c*) In 3:18-23, we witness the characteristically poignant Jewish negotiation between sadness and hope. Verse 18 asserts that hope is gone. In verse 21, hope reappears, for in verses 22-23, Israel voices its three great terms of buoyancy — steadfast love, mercy, and faithfulness. These words do not here triumph, but they hover in the very midst of Israel's sadness and refuse to be pushed out of the artistic discernment of the Jews. Because the sadness is fully voiced, one can see the com-

---

17. See Delbert R. Hillers, *Lamentations: A New Translation with Introduction and Commentary*, Anchor Bible 7A (Garden City, N.Y.: Doubleday, 1972), xl–xli.

munity begin to move in its buoyancy, but not too soon. This practice of *buoyance through sadness* is one many pastors know about in situations of "bereavement." We have, however, not seen that the category of bereavement operates communally as well, concerning the loss of our "great days" as a superpower with an economy to match or as a church, which now tends to be a "has-been."

The sadness of Jews in exile can of course grow much more shrill. It is then not a far move from lament to rage, as classically expressed in Psalm 137. The psalm is of course an embarrassment to us because of its "lethal" ending. And yet every pastor knows about folk with exactly such rage and for exactly the same reasons. We seethe, as did they, over our unfair losses that leave us displaced and orphaned. With such texts, the church need not engage in pious cover-up or false assurance. This psalm in its rage is an act of "catching up" with new reality. If Zion's songs are to be sung, it will be a long, long way from all old "Zions." The psalmist is beginning to engage that tough but undeniable reality.

2. The utterance of the terms "forgotten" and "forsaken" in Lamentations 5:20 (see the same verbs and same sentiment in Isa. 49:14) suggests that the exiles are like "a motherless child," that is, an abandoned, vulnerable orphan. Exile is an act of being orphaned, and many folk now sense themselves in that status. There is no sure home, no old family place, no recognizable family food. I suggest the theme of *rootlessness*, as though we do not belong anywhere. The enormous popularity of Alex Haley's *Roots* came about, I suggest, not because of fascination with or guilt about slavery, but because of resonance with the need to recover connection and genealogy. (On a less dramatic plane, it is astonishing how many people look to Salt Lake City in order to have the Mormons find their ancestors.)

Exiles need to take with them old habits, old customs, old memories, old photographs. The scriptural resources for such uprooted folk, I suggest, are the genealogies that have seemed to us boring and therefore have been skipped over.[18] We have skipped over them, I imagine,

---

18. For a critical understanding of the function of the genealogies, see Marshall D. Johnson, *The Purpose of the Biblical Genealogies: With Special Reference to the Genealogies of Jesus,* Society for New Testament Studies Monograph Series 8 (London: Cambridge University Press, 1969); and Robert R. Wilson, *Genealogy and History in the Biblical World* (New Haven: Yale University Press, 1977).

either because we thought those old names were not intrinsically interesting or because we thought they referenced some family other
than our own. The recovery of these genealogies could indeed give
an index of the mothers and fathers who have risked before us, who
have hoped before us, and who continue even now to believe in us
and hope for us. The genealogies might be useful in the recovery of
baptism because in that act, we join a new family. And we are like any
new in-law at a first family reunion, when we meet all the weird un-
cles and solicitous aunts, who seem like an undifferentiated mass until
they are linked with lots of stories.[19] After the stories are known, then
the list becomes meaningful and is simply shorthand that makes and
keeps the stories available. Two easy access points for such genealogy are (a) the Matthean genealogy, which includes some of our most
scandalous mothers (Matt. 1:13–17), and (b) the recital in Hebrews
11 of all our family "by faith."

The texts serve to overcome the isolation of the orphan and our
sense of motherless existence, by giving us the names of mothers and
fathers and by situating us in a "communion of saints," who are the
living dead who continue to watch over us. I suggest that if the ge-
nealogical indices are well handled, they become a way to recover old
narratives that contextualize our present faith. When well done, moreover, local congregations can extend the list, not only of members of
their own congregation, but of folk known publicly, beyond the congregation, who have risked for and shaped faith. It is inevitable that
with this evocation of gratitude to those on the list, we enter our
names on the same list with a sense of accountability and begin to
understand what it might mean to have our own names written in
"the book of life."[20]

3. The most obvious reality and greatest threat to exiles is the
power of despair. On the one hand, everything for which we have
worked is irretrievably lost. On the other hand, we are helpless in this
circumstance and are fated here forever. In ancient Israel, this despair
of a theological kind is rooted in two failures of faith. First, Israel
doubts *God's fidelity,* that is, God's capacity to care and remember (cf.

---

19. Wonderful examples of the way such stories and such characters people imagination are
the biographical statements by Russell Baker, *Growing Up* (New York: New American Library-
Dutton, 1983) and *The Good Times* (New York: New American Library-Dutton, 1991).

20. Cf. Exod. 32:32–33; Isa. 4:3; 56:5; Dan. 12:1; Rev. 3:5; 13:8; 17:8; 20:12, 15; 21:27.

Lam. 5:20, quoted in Isa. 49:14). Second, Israel doubts *God's power* to save, even if God remembers (cf. Isa. 50:2; 59:1). On both counts, Israel has concluded that in its exile, it is without a God who makes any difference and is therefore hopelessly in the grip of the perpetrators of exile.

The scriptural resource against this despair is voiced especially in Isaiah 40–55. This is a text well known to us, if for no other reason than that Handel has made it available to us. Very often, however, critical study of this text has focused on distracting questions, like "Who is the Suffering Servant?" Leaders of exilic communities in despair, as I suspect some of us are, would do better to focus on the primary intent of the poetry, namely, that God's powerful resolve is to transform the debilitating reality of exile. Of the rich resources in this poetry, we may identify especially four motifs voiced as hope against despair:

It is this poetry that transforms the word "gospel" (*bsr*) into a theological term. In 40:9 and 52:7, the "good news" is that Yahweh has triumphed over the power of exile, that is, over Babylonian gods (cf. 46:1–4) and over Babylonian royal power (47:1–11). As a result, Israel's self-definition need not be derived from that harsh, seemingly permanent regime.

It is II Isaiah's words that explode the faith of Israel into creation faith (cf. 40:12–17; 42:5; 44:24). Now the scope of God's saving power is not a nickel-and-dime operation in Israel, but the whole of global reality is viewed as a resource whereby God's transformative action is mobilized on behalf of this little, needy community. In this poetry, creation is not an end in itself but an instrument of rescue. Israel is urged to "think big" and to "sing big" about the forces of life at work on its behalf.

Speeches of judgment show God, as construed by this poet, engaged in a heavy-handed dispute with Babylonian gods in order to delegitimate their claims and to establish the proper claims of Yahwistic faith (41:21–29; 44:6–7; 45:20–21). The purpose of such rhetorical action is to give Israel "spine," to enable Israel not to give up its covenantal identity for the sake of its ostensive masters. That is, Israel is invited to *chutzpah* in holding to its own peculiar identity.

This defiant speech against the other, phony gods is matched by an affirmative tenderness expressed in salvation oracles (41:13, 14–

16; 43:1–5). Rolf Rendtorff and Rainer Albertz have noticed that "creation language" is used in salvation oracles, not to refer to "the creation of the world," but for the creation of Israel, who is God's treasured creature.[21] As is often recognized, Isaiah 43:1–5 articulates something like baptismal phrasing: "I have called you by name, you are mine." That baptismal language, however, is cast in creation speech forms.

This combination of defiance and tenderness indicates that Israel's seemingly helpless present is teeming with liberating intentionality. Israel is expected, in this poetry, to cease its mesmerized commitment to the rulers of this age (here Babylon), who thrive on the despair of Israel, and to receive through this poetry the freedom of imagination to act "as" a people headed "home."[22] In our contemporary circumstance of ministry, I suggest that despair is our defining pathology that robs the church of missional energy and of stewardship generosity. The poet who uttered these words has dared to voice an originary option against all the visible evidence. But then, faith is precisely and characteristically "the assurance of things hoped for, the conviction of things not seen" (Heb. 11:1). As long as the exiles hope for nothing and are convinced of nothing unseen, it is guaranteed that they will stay in thrall to Babylon. The poet refuses such a pitiful, shameful abandonment of identity.

4. Exile is an experience of *profaned absence*. That is, the "absence of God" is not only a personal, emotional sense but a public, institutional awareness that "the glory has departed." In ancient Israel this sense had to do with the destruction of the temple, the departure of God from Jerusalem (cf. Ezek. 9–10) so that God "had no place," and the abusive handling of temple vessels so that the very "vehicles for God" were treated like a tradeable commodity.[23]

In our time, it is clear that what have long been treasured symbols are treated lightly or with contempt. (I suspect that this is what is

---

21. Rolf Rendtorff, "Die theologische Stellung des Schöpfungsglaubens bei Deuterojesaja," *Zeitschrift für Theologie und Kirche* 51 (1954): 3–13; Rainer Albertz, *Weltschöpfung und Menschenschöpfung: Untersucht bei Deuterojesaja, Hiob und in den Psalmen*, Calwer Theologische Mongraphien 3 (Stuttgart: Calwer Verlag, 1974).

22. On "as" as "the copula of imagination," see Garrett Green, *Imagining God: Theology and the Religious Imagination* (San Francisco: Harper & Row, 1989), 73, 140, and passim.

23. Ackroyd, "The Temple Vessels: A Continuity Theme," shows how the temple vessels can be narrated to report a complete and decisive break in historical continuity or, conversely, can be used to enact continuity in the midst of enormous discontinuity.

entailed in the great passion generated by flag burning and bra burning and by such acts of defiance against "sacred order.") Very many people have concluded with chagrin that "nothing is sacred anymore." With the absence of God, larger "meanings" become impossible. And because God is absent, we become increasingly selfish and brutalizing because without God, "everything is possible." (No doubt popular, right-wing religion trades effectively on this sense of loss.)

Unfortunately, critical scholarship (and especially Protestant usage) has neglected the texts that pertain to the "crisis of presence," which are found especially in the Priestly (P) texts of the Pentateuch.[24] With our deep-seated Protestant resistance to any sacramentalism that sounds automatic and/or routine, the P texts have been treated by us with a rather consistent lack of interest, if not disdain.

It is important for us, in our exilic situation, to renotice that these texts constitute a major pastoral response to the exilic crisis of absence. I suggest that these texts might be useful resources for ministry if we understand them as a recovery of sacrament as a way to "host the holy" in a context of profane absence. That is, the priests had no inclination, or found it impossible, to affirm that God was everywhere loose in the exile of Babylon. Indeed, a case could be made in priestly perception that God would refuse to be available in such a miserable context as Babylon. Where then might God be? The answer is, in the sacramental life of Israel, so that God becomes a counterpresence to Babylonian profanation. The reason for coming to "the holy place" is to come into "the presence," which is everywhere else precluded in this exile that is under hostile management.

I suggest three aspects of this recovery of the sacramental, plus a footnote. (*a*) Central to the sacramental life of Israel was *circumcision* (cf. Gen. 17). To be sure, that powerful cultic act is profoundly patriarchal. In the exile, however, it becomes a rich and larger metaphor for faith (cf. Deut. 10:16; 30:6; Jer. 4:4). Moreover, the "marking" of circumcision is transposed in Christian practice into baptism, which, like circumcision, is a mark of distinctiveness. It distinguishes its subjects

---

24. On the general theme and problem of presence, see Samuel Terrien, *The Elusive Presence: Toward a New Biblical Theology,* Religious Perspectives 26 (New York: Harper & Row, 1978). More specifically on presence as understood in the Priestly tradition, see Robert B. Coote and David Robert Ord, *In the Beginning: Creation and the Priestly History* (Minneapolis: Fortress, 1991), esp. chaps. 9–11.

from the definitions of the empire, even if the Babylonians cannot see it. (*b*) *Sabbath* emerges as a primal act of faith in exile. I understand the sabbath to be a quiet but uncompromising refusal to be defined by the production system of Babylon so that life is regularly and with discipline enacted as a trusted gift and not as a frantic achievement. (*c*) Most important, the *tabernacle* is an imaginative effort to form a special place where God's holiness can be properly hosted and therefore counted upon (Exod. 25–31; 35–40; cf. Ezek. 40–48 on an exilic concern for cultic presence). I am not convinced that this text of Exodus 25–31 and 35–40 describes any concrete, practiced reality in exilic Israel. It may be nothing more than a textual fantasy. Nonetheless, it is a fantasy about presence, about the willingness of the exodus God to sojourn midst this displaced people of the wilderness. While God is thus willing to occupy and visit a disestablished people, the presence of God is not casual or haphazard. It requires discipline and care that is almost punctilious.

It is thoroughly biblical to attend to modes of presence that are visible (material, physical) so that the whole of presence is not verbal (or sermonic). I understand the reasons why conventional Protestantism has avoided such modes of thought and practice. Such a resistance was necessary in order to break the terrible and destructive power of the old sacramentalism in the sixteenth century. It is the case, however, that our present "exilic" crisis is not marked by a threat of "popish sacramentalism," as in the sixteenth century. Our threat rather is a technological emptiness that is filled by the liturgies of consumerism and commoditization. And the issue in our own context is whether holy presence can be received, imagined, and practiced in ways that counteract that powerful, debilitating ideology. It is clear that the Letter to the Hebrews (chaps. 7–10) does not flinch from thinking christologically in terms of tabernacle presence. I suspect that for exiles, a verbal presence by itself is too thin, which is why the Priestly materials came to dominate the canon. It is also why Reformed faith in the magisterial tradition may want to make ecumenical moves to reengage the very sacramentalism it scuttled. Exiles who live in a profaned context have a deep need to "touch and handle" things unseen.

5. Exile is an experience of *moral incongruity*. That is, the displacement and destructiveness of exile make one aware that the terrible fate

of displacement is more massive than can be explained in terms of moral symmetry. The classic biblical response to exile is that exile is punishment from God for the violation of torah. Such a guilt-focused interpretation does indeed keep the world morally coherent and reliable. But at enormous cost! The cost of protecting God's moral reliability is to take the blame for very large disorders. This sense of blame, in my judgment, exacts too high a cost for moral symmetry and so produces the practical problem of theodicy, the awareness that this "evil" cannot be explained by or contained in our "fault." Something else besides our "fault" is loose and at work in the destabilizing of our world.[25]

In the Old Testament, the problem of theodicy, that is, the thought that God is implicated in a morally incoherent world, surfaces in the Book of Job. While the Book of Job cannot be securely tied to the context of exile, most scholars believe it belongs there, and many believe it is a direct and intentional response to the oversimplification of retribution theology.[26]

Mutatis mutandis, the problem of theodicy belongs appropriately to our own exilic circumstance. If exile be understood as "the failure of the established church," it is difficult to think that this failure is "our fault," for the forces of secularism are larger than we are, and it does not much good to blame somebody. If exile be understood as "the failure of the white, male, Western hegemony," it is difficult to take the blame as a white male, even if one is generically implicated. The Book of Job is able to entertain in any exile, including ours, that something more is at work than fault so that our circumstance of exile is not easily reduced to moral symmetry.

I think that the honest surfacing of this issue of theodicy, in Joban terms, would be a liberating act among us. It is an act that fully acknowledges moral asymmetry, that does not reduce reality to "scorekeeping," that refuses to accept all the blame, and that dares

---

25. Paul Ricoeur, *The Symbolism of Evil* (Boston: Beacon, 1967), 255–60, traces the way in which Genesis portrays human persons as both *perpetrators* and *victims*. Already in that narrative, which is characteristically read as though it concerned only fault, Israel has carefully nuanced the ambiguity in social experience.

26. See Samuel Terrien, "Job as a Sage," in *The Sage in Israel and the Ancient Near East*, ed. John G. Gammie and Leo G. Perdue (Winona Lake, Ind.: Eisenbrauns, 1990), 231–42; and Rainer Albertz, "The Sage Adds Pious Wisdom in the Book of Job: The Friends' Perspective," in ibid., 243–61.

to entertain the unsettled thought of God's failure. In the poem of
Job, both the terrible indictment of God (9:13–24) and the confident
self-affirmation of Job (chaps. 29–31) prepare the way for the whirlwind, which blows away all moral issues (38:1–42:6). In the extremity
of exile, I believe it would be an important pastoral gain to have the
whirlwind obliterate and blow away many of our all-consuming moral
questions. In the poem of Job, the questions of failure, fault, blame,
and guilt simply evaporate. We are invited to a larger vista of mystery
that contains wild and threatening dimensions of faith. The poem
extricates Israel from the barrenness of moral explanation and justification and thinks instead of dangerous trust and affirmation in a
context where we cannot see our way through. The world of Job is
filled with wondrous crocodiles (41:1–34) and hippopotamus (40:15–
24) along with cunning evil, deep, unanswered questions and vigorous
doxology.

It is also a world where, through the dismay, gifts are given and
life inexplicably goes on (42:7–17). If Job be misunderstood as an intellectual enterprise, it may cut the nerve of faith. But if it be taken
as a pastoral opportunity to explode petty, narcissistic categories for a
larger field of mystery, it might indeed enable exiles to embrace their
self-concern and then to move past it to a larger, more dangerous
dimension of living in an unresolvable and inexplicable world where
God's mystery overrides all our moral programs.

6. The danger in exile is to become so preoccupied with self that
one cannot get outside one's self to rethink, reimagine, and redescribe
larger reality. Self-preoccupation seldom yields energy, courage, or
freedom. In ancient Israel, one of the strategies for coping shrewdly
and responsibly beyond self was the narratives of defiance and cunning that enjoined exiles, not to confront their harsh overlords
directly, but to negotiate knowingly between faith and the pressures
of "reality."[27]

If we can get past difficult critical problems, we may take some
such narratives as models and invitations for living freely, danger-
ously, and tenaciously in a world where faith does not have its own
way. Smith shows how these narratives perform a crucial strategic

---

27. Concerning these narratives, I am primarily informed by Smith, *The Religion of the
Landless*, 153–78.

function and includes in his analysis the tales of Daniel, Joseph, and Esther. We may comment briefly upon these resources: (*a*) The story of Joseph concerns the capacity of an Israelite to cooperate fully with the established regime (perhaps too fully) but to maintain at the same time an edge of discernment that permits him to look out for his folk. He does not fully adopt the "reality" defined by his overlords. (*b*) The tale of Esther shows a courageous Jew willing and able to outflank established power, to gain not only honor for herself but well-being for her people. (*c*) The story of Daniel shows a young man pressed into the civil service of the empire, able to exercise authority in the empire precisely because he maintained a sense of self rooted quite outside the empire.

This practice of narrative admits of no easy "Christ against culture" model but recognizes the requirement of an endlessly cunning, risky process of negotiation. Such negotiations may seem to purists to be too accommodationist. And to accommodationists, they may seem excessively scrupulous. If, however, assimilation into the dominant culture is a major threat for exiles, the lead characters of these narratives do not forget who they are, with whom they belong, nor the God whom they serve. I imagine many baptized exiles must live such a life of endless negotiation. These narratives might name and clarify the process and tilt self-perception toward membership in the faithful community. The stunning characters in these narratives are indeed "bilingual," knowing the speech of the empire and being willing to use it but never forgetting the cadences of their "mother tongue."

IV

It is clear that "exile" is a rich and supple metaphor. As the biblical writers turned the metaphor of exile in various and imaginative directions, so may we. Note well, I have made no argument about the one-to-one match between metaphor and reality. I have proposed only that this metaphor mediates our experience to us in fresh ways and gives access to scriptural resources in equally fresh ways.

There are two by-products in the utilization of a countermetaphor that I will mention. On the one hand, pondering this metaphor helps us think again about a rich variety of metaphors in Scripture that can function as a kaleidoscope to let us see our life and faith in various dimensions, aspects, angles, and contexts. Such an exercise may move us past a single, frozen metaphor that we take as a permanent given. On the other hand, the availability of a countermetaphor that opens us to a plurality of metaphors helps us notice that our usual, "taken for granted" world is also a metaphorical construct, even if an unrecognized or unacknowledged one. That is, postmodern awareness helps us to consider that there is no "given reality" behind our several constructs, but even our presumed given reality is itself a rhetorical construct, whether of the cold war or consumer capitalism or the "free world" or the male hegemony or whatever.[28] An awareness of this reality about "world" and about "self" opens the way to liminality, which permits transformation of all those "givens."[29]

In the argument I have made, there are important interpretive issues to be considered by the preacher. I suggest that the Bible be understood as a set of models (paradigms) of reality made up of images situated in and contextualized by narratives.[30] These narrative renderings of reality in the Bible (as elsewhere) are not factual reportage but are inevitably artistic constructs that stand a distance from any "fact" and are filtered through interest of a political kind. I think it a major gain to see that the Bible in its several models is an artistic, rhetorical proposal of reality that seeks to persuade (convert) to an alternative sense of God, world, neighbor, and self.

As there are interpretive implications to the argument I have made, so there are also crucial ecclesial implications in construing life through the metaphor of exile. This literary, rhetorical focus invites the baptismal community to construe its place in the world differ-

---

28. Green, *Imagining God*, 41–60, has taught me the most concerning the fact that our "givens" are dependent upon paradigmatic construals of reality. On the cruciality of rhetoric for reality, see the suggestive interface of religion and rhetoric suggested by Wayne C. Booth, "Rhetoric and Religion: Are They Essentially Wedded?" in *Radical Pluralism and Truth: David Tracy and the Hermeneutics of Religion*, ed. Werner G. Jeanrond and Jennifer L. Rike (New York: Crossroad, 1991), 62–80.

29. On the use of the notion of liminality from Victor Turner in the interest of religious transformation, see Urban T. Holmes, "The Priest as Enchanter," in *To Be a Priest: Perspectives on Vocation and Ordination*, ed. Robert E. Terwilliger and Urban T. Holmes (San Francisco: Harper & Row, 1975), 173–81; and Marchita B. Mauck, "The Liminal Space of Ritual and Art," in *The Bent World: Essays on Religion and Culture*, ed. John R. May (Chico, Calif.: Scholars, 1981), 149–57.

30. See Roy Schafer, *Retelling a Life: Narration and Dialogue in Psychoanalysis* (New York: Basic, 1992), esp. chap. 2.

ently and, I imagine, faithfully.[31] The engagement with this metaphor may deliver pastors and people from magisterial notions of being (or needing to be) chaplains for the establishment and guardians of stable public forms of life.

I understand the liberty given through this metaphor quite practically and concretely. As the preacher stands up to preach among the exiles, the primal task (given this metaphor) concerns the narration and nurture of a counteridentity, the enactment of the power of hope in a season of despair, and the assertion of a deep definitional freedom from the pathologies, coercions, and seductions that govern our society. The preacher is called upon, not to do all the parts of public policy and public morality, but to give the spine, resolve, courage, energy, and freedom that belong to a counteridentity.

As the congregation listens and participates in this odd construal of reality, the metaphor might also make a decisive difference in the listening. The working woman or man knows that "it is a jungle out there" and that one without a resilient, resistant identity can indeed be eaten alive. The teenager off to school is in the rat race of success and popularity, leave alone competence and adequacy. And now every man, woman, and child is invited to a zone of freedom that the dominant culture cannot erode. That zone of freedom is grounded in what the baptized know:

- that our sense of *loss and sadness* is serious and honorable and that one need not prop up or engage in denial;

- that our *rootedness* enables us to belong so that we are not swept away by every wind of doctrine, every market seduction, or every economic coercion, knowing who we are;

- that the promises of the Creator surge in our life and in our world so that the *manipulatable despair* of the hopeless, which turns folk into commodity consumers, is not the live edge of our existence;

- that there is a *holy, awesome presence* that persists against the emptied profanation of promiscuous economic and lustful sex-

31. See William H. Willimon, *Peculiar Speech: Preaching to the Baptized* (Grand Rapids: Eerdmans, 1992).

uality and that true *desire* is for the presence that overrides all of
our trivialized desires, which are now robbed of authority;

- that the world is *not morally coherent;* that there is a deep incongruity in which we live, which we need not resolve, explain, nor
  deny; and that a raw, ragged openness is linked to the awesome
  reality of God's holiness;

- that we are always about to be domesticated and that we
  have these *narrative models of resistance, defiance, and negotiation,* which remind us that there is more to life than conformist
  obedience or shameful accommodation. We know the names of
  those who have faced with freedom the trouble that is caused
  by faith.

There is nothing in this faith model of "sectarian withdrawal," the
kind of which Hauerwas and Willimon are often accused.[32] The baptized do indeed each day find themselves finally in the presence of
those who preside over the exile, that is, in the presence of "Babylonians." They are unavoidable, even in this model, or especially in this
model. This baptismal identity is not designed for a ghetto existence.
It is rather intended for full participation in the life of the dominant culture, albeit with a sense of subversiveness that gives unnerving
freedom.

Jeremiah knew about the dangers of withdrawal from dominant
culture. For that reason, in his letter to the exiles, the prophet
encourages the exiles with amazing, endlessly problematic words:[33]

> But seek the welfare (*shalom*) of the city where I have sent you
> into exile, and pray to the LORD on its behalf, for in its welfare
> (*shalom*) you will find your welfare (*shalom*). (Jer. 29:7)

There is no "separate peace" for exiles, no private deals with God, no
permitted withdrawal from the affairs of the empire. The only *shalom*

---

32. The critique often leveled against Willimon and Hauerwas, that they are sectarian, is
driven by the long-established categories of H. Richard Niebuhr concerning Christ and culture.
It is now clear that those older categories are no longer adequate for the actual situation of the
church in Western culture and that a critique must be made of Niebuhr's typology. See, for
example, Robert E. Webber, *The Church in the World: Opposition, Tension, or Transformation?*
Academie Books (Grand Rapids: Zondervan, 1986), 261–78 and passim.

33. Smith, *The Religion of the Landless,* 127–38, provides a most discerning study of the letter
concerning the "social psychology of a group under stress."

these troubled Jews would know is the *shalom* wrought for Babylon. The letter implies that the exiled community of Jews can indeed impact Babylon with *shalom* through its active concern and prayer, but only as the community knows that it is not Babylon. The distance from Babylon makes possible an impacting nearness to Babylon.

Finally, but not too soon, the preacher's theme for exiles is homecoming. The home promised to the exiles, however, is not any nostalgic return to yesteryear, for that home is irreversibly gone. Rather, the home for which the exiles yearn and toward which they hope is the "kingdom of God," an arena in which God's good intention is decisive. The New Testament struggles to speak concretely about that realm and can do so only indirectly and by allusion, for that realm lies beyond all our known categories.

It is no stretch to link *homecoming* to *gospel* to *kingdom*. The linkage is already made in Isaiah 40–55 and in Ezekiel 37:1–14. It is telling that Karl Barth speaks of the "obedience of the Son of God" under the rubric of "The Way of the Son of God into a Far Country."[34] The textual allusion is of course to the prodigal son, though Barth's accent is on the "emptying and humiliation" of Jesus, as in Philippians 2:5–11.[35] Conversely, in speaking of the exaltation of Jesus, Barth writes of "the Homecoming of the Son of Man."[36] An important critique may be made of Barth's usage, for it reflects his characteristic transcendentalism, whereby the course of human existence is by definition exile. It is my intention to suggest that the metaphor of exile-homecoming, which Barth handles christologically and which Buber handles philosophically, be understood among us ecclesiologically with reference to the concrete realities of economic, politics, and social relations.

Consider, then, what it means to be exiles awaiting and hoping for homecoming to the kingdom of God! In the Bible, the image of the "kingdom of God" is stitched together by narratives of miracle and wonder, whereby God does concrete acts of transformation that the world judges to be impossible. The "kingdom" is a time and place and

---

34. Karl Barth, *Church Dogmatics*, vol. 4, pt. 2 (Edinburgh: T. & T. Clark, 1956), no. 59, 157–210.

35. Ibid., 180–83, 188–94.

36. Karl Barth, *Church Dogmatics*, vol. 4, pt. 2 (Edinburgh: T. & T. Clark, 1958), no, 64, 20–154. On the parable of Luke 15:11–32, see pp. 21–25.

context in which God's "impossibilities" for life, joy, and wholeness
are all made possible and available.[37] In the meantime, the waiting,
hoping exiles are fixed upon these impossibilities. In so doing, the exiles refuse the world's verdict on the impossibilities, and as a result,
they pay less heed and allegiance to the world's wearisome possibilities. The alternative to this subversive entry into the world is to accept
the world's possibilities as the only chance for the future. Such a decision rejects the miracles of God and so enters endlessly into the
seductive land of exile. Failing the countervision of the gospel, we
will no doubt "labor for that which does not satisfy" (Isa. 55:2).

---

37. On the "impossibilities" of the kingdom, see Walter Brueggemann, "'Impossibility' and
Epistemology in the Faith Traditions of Abraham and Sarah (Genesis 18:1–15)," *Zeitschrift für
die alttestamentliche Wissenschaft* 94 (1982): 615–34.

2

CADENCES
WHICH REDESCRIBE
Speech among Exiles

Walter Brueggemann

Exile, that is, social, cultural displacement, is not primarily geographical, but it is liturgical and symbolic.[1] This was the case with the Jews in exile in the sixth century B.C.E., as it is in our Western culture presently. In defining exile, Alan Mintz writes: "The catastrophic element in events [of exile] is defined as the power to shatter the existing paradigms of meaning, especially as regards the bonds between God and the people of Israel."[2] In such a situation where "paradigms of meaning" are shattered, it is clear that exiles must pay careful and sustained attention to speech because it requires inordinately disciplined and imaginative speech to move through the shattering to newly voiced meaning. Mintz suggests that in exile, the primal speakers (poets) attempt "first to *represent the catastrophe* and then to *reconstruct, replace, or redraw the threatened paradigm of meaning*, and thereby make creative survival possible."[3]

I find Paul Ricoeur's phrasing a useful way to understand what is required and what is possible for speech in such situations. Ricoeur speaks in terms of "limit experiences," which permit and require "limit expressions."[4] "Limit experiences" are those in which all conventional

---

1. On my understanding of exile as a useful metaphor for the contemporary crisis of the U.S. church, see Walter Brueggemann, "Disciplines of Readiness," in *Occasional Paper No. 1*, Theology and Worship Unit, Presbyterian Church (U.S.A.), Louisville, 1989; and "Preaching to Exiles," *Journal for Preachers* 16 (Pentecost 1993): 3–15.

2. Alan Mintz, *Hurban: Responses to Catastrophe in Hebrew Literature* (New York: Columbia University Press, 1984), x. I am indebted to Tod Linafelt for this most remarkable reference.

3. Mintz, *Hurban*, 2. I have added the emphasis.

4. Paul Ricoeur, "Biblical Hermeneutics," *Semeia* 4 (1975): 107–45.

descriptions and explanations are inadequate. When one is pushed experientially to such extremity, one cannot continue to mouth commonplaces but is required to utter something "odd."[5] The "odd" limit expression is in language that effectively "redescribes" reality away from and apart from all usual assumptions about reality.[6] Thus such speech invites the speaker and the listener into a world that neither had known before this utterance.

It is clear that in exile, while something utterly new must be uttered, that is, not contained within or regulated by past utterance, this daring speech that evokes newness nonetheless employs in fresh ways speech that is already known and trusted. In order to serve as "redescription," however, the already trusted speech must be uttered in daring, venturesome ways that intensify, subvert, and amaze.

By utilizing the theme of exile as an analogue by which to describe (redescribe?) our current social situation in the West, I suggest that our loss of the white, male, Western, colonial hegemony, which is deeply displacing for us, is indeed a limit experience, whereby we are pushed to the edge of our explanatory and coping powers. Such experience requires limit expression, and such a consideration belongs in an article for preachers precisely because preachers in such a limit experience have the obligation and the possibility of being the very ones who can give utterance both to "represent the catastrophe" and to "reconstruct, replace, or redraw" the paradigms of meaning that will permit "creative survival." I suggest that preaching is now nothing less than that twofold task.

In what follows I will consider four examples of limit expression that were utilized in that ancient exile of sixth-century Jews in order that their limit experience of displacement could be embraced and moved through. My thought is that there are clues here for our own speech practice in a time of acute displacement and bewilderment.

Lamentation and Complaint

The first task among exiles is to "represent the catastrophe," to state what is happening by way of loss in vivid images so that the loss can

---

5. The "odd speech" with which Ricoeur deals includes proclamatory sayings, proverbs, and parables. Cf. "Biblical Hermeneutics," 109–18.

6. Ricoeur, "Biblical Hermeneutics," 31, 127, and passim.

be named by its right name and so that it can be publicly faced in the depth of its negativity. Such naming and facing permit the loss to be addressed to God, who is implicated in the loss as less than faithful in a context seen to be one of fickleness and failure. Such speech requires enough candor to dare to utter the torrent of sensitivities that cluster, such as pain, loss, grief, shame, and rage. For this, of course, this ancient Jewish community found its best speech by appeal to the liturgic tradition of *lamentation* (which expresses sadness) and *complaint* (which expresses indignation).[7]

The richest, most extreme statement of sadness, punctuated by loss, helplessness, and vulnerability, is the Book of Lamentations.[8] It is not much studied or used among us, no doubt because it has seemed so remote from our cultural situation. If, however, we are now in a new situation of profound loss, as I have suggested, this poetry could be for us an important "speech resource." The little Book of Lamentations consists of five extended poems of grief over the destruction of Jerusalem (for which I have suggested as an analogue the loss of our accustomed privilege and certitude). In the first poem (chap. 1), the bereft city of Jerusalem is "like a widow," abandoned, shamed, vulnerable, subject to abuse, without an advocate or defender (1:1). The recurring theme of the abandonment of Jerusalem is expressed as "no one to comfort her" (vv. 2, 9, 16, 17), "no resting place" (v. 3), "no pasture" (v. 6), "no one to help" (v. 7). The imagery is of a woman overwhelmed with tears, under assault, and subject to abuse.[9] While there is in 3:21–33 a powerful statement of hope and confidence, the collection of Lamentations ends with a sense of "forsakenness":

---

7. The basic book on lamentation is Claus Westermann, *Praise and Lament in the Psalms* (Atlanta: John Knox, 1981).

8. Mintz, *Hurban*, 17–48, has the most suggestive discussion of the Book of Lamentations known to me. The most reliable commentary is Delbert R. Hillers, *Lamentations: A New Translation with Introduction and Commentary*, Anchor Bible 7A (Garden City, N.Y.: Doubleday, 1972).

9. Mintz, *Hurban*, 24, most helpfully discerns what is at stake in this particular imagery:

The serviceableness of the image of Jerusalem as an abandoned fallen woman lies in the precise register of pain it articulates. An image of death would have purveyed the false comfort of finality; the dead have finished with suffering and their agony can be evoked only in retrospect. The raped and defiled woman who survives, on the other hand, is a living witness to a pain that knows no release. It is similarly the perpetualness of her situation that comes through most forcefully when Zion is pictured as a woman crying bitterly alone in the night with tears wetting her face (1:2). The cry seems to ululate permanently in the night; the tear forever falls to the cheek. It is a matter not just of lingering suffering but of continuing exposure to victimization.

> Why have you *forgotten* us completely?
> Why have you *forsaken* us these many days?
> (Lam. 5:20, emphasis added)

This same sense of being "forgotten" is evident in the more abrasive and indignant complaint of Psalm 74, where the poet is more aggressive in describing to God the situation of dismay and in pressing God to act.[10] The poem provides for God a play-by-play of what "your foes" have done to "your holy place" (Ps. 74:4; cf. vv. 4–9). It then moves to a doxology (see below), recalling to God God's own powerful miracles of the past (vv. 12–17). These concern God's sovereign rule over all of creation and God's capacity to bring life out of chaos. By juxtaposing the present calamity of the temple and God's glorious past, the poem makes intercession that God should now act, both to defeat the impious enemies and to ensure that the downtrodden are not "put to shame" (v. 21; cf. vv. 18–23). One is struck in this psalm with the directness of speech, the candor about the current trouble (which is catastrophic), and the vigor with which God is expected to act in fidelity.

Through both the lamentation and the psalm of complaint, the catastrophic is vividly "represented," to make it palpable to God as it is to the community. My suggestion, insofar as our current Western dismay is a parallel to this ancient travesty, is that a primary pastoral task is to voice the felt loss, indignation, and bewilderment that are among us. The reason extreme imagery is required is that the speech must cut through the enormous self-deception of political-economic euphemism. For the truth is that the old, settled advantage in the world upon which we have counted is over and gone, as over and gone as was Jerusalem's temple. Sadness, pain, and indignation are not inappropriate responses to the loss, either then or now. They require abrasive, insistent speech to be available, and ancient Israel gives us a script for our own daring "representation" of the trouble.

---

10. The contrast between the Book of Lamentations and Psalm 74 is the difference between "lament" and "complaint." Erhard Gerstenberger, "Jeremiah's Complaints: Observations on Jer. 15:10–21," *Journal of Biblical Literature* 82 (1963): 405 n. 50, draws the distinction nicely: "A lament bemoans a tragedy which cannot be reversed, while a complaint entreats God for help in the midst of tribulation." The distinction and interrelatedness of the two are nicely expressed in German, *Klage* and *Anklage*.

Assurance

In the laments and complaints, Israel speaks to God. Israel takes the initiative in rightly naming its displacement to God. In times of debilitating dismay, it is the one who experiences the dismay who must courageously come to speech.[11] This is abundantly clear in the speech of ancient Israel. But Israel's limit expressions are not restricted to the voice of Israel. The voice of Yahweh also sounds in the daring rhetoric of the exile, precisely in the context where Israel had sensed its abandonment by God. Indeed, in the poetry of II Isaiah, God acknowledges that God has been silent too long and will now break that silence in powerful speech. God says,

> For a long time I have held my peace,
> I have kept still and restrained myself;
> Now I will cry out like a woman in labor,
> I will gasp and pant. (Isa. 42:14; cf. 62:1)[12]

In the "salvation oracles" of II Isaiah, Israel hears the classic assurance that God is present with and for Israel, even in its dismay and displacement. Most precisely and succinctly, this oracle of assurance asserts on God's lips, "Fear not, for I am with you" (cf. Isa. 41:13, 14; 43:1–5; 44:8; Jer. 30:10–11).[13] Joseph Sittler among others has seen that this speech is closely paralleled to the way a parent reassures a child who has had a nightmare.[14] Such parental assurance is indeed a "redescription." Indeed, this assurance is a nightmare-ending speech, for it asserts a caring presence that is trusted enough and powerful enough to override the sense of absence evoked by the exile. Now, in this utterance, what had seemed to be a place of absence is known to be a place of presence, thereby invested with great potential for life.

---

11. On the cruciality of coming to speech, see Elaine Scarry, *The Body in Pain: The Making and Unmaking of the World* (New York: Oxford University Press, 1985); and Judith Lewis Herman, *Trauma and Recovery: The Aftermath of Violence — From Domestic Abuse to Political Terror* (New York: Basic, 1992).

12. There is a powerful play of imagery in the relation between Jerusalem as an abused widow and Yahweh as a restless woman about to give birth.

13. The most complete study of the genre is by Edgar W. Conrad, *Fear Not Warrior: A Study of 'al tira' Pericopes in the Hebrew Scriptures*, Brown Judaic Studies 75 (Chico, Calif.: Scholars, 1985).

14. Joseph Sittler, *Grace and Gravity: Reflections and Provocations* (Minneapolis: Augsburg, 1986), 99–100. See the more comprehensive discussion by Gail R. O'Day, "Toward a Biblical Theology of Preaching," in *Listening to the Word: Studies in Honor of Fred B. Craddock*, ed. Gail R. O'Day and Thomas G. Long (Nashville: Abingdon, 1993), 17–32.

While the salvation oracle proper is highly stylized, Claus Westermann has seen that there are great variations on the theme of assurance expressed in a variety of forms, including what he calls "assurance of salvation," "announcement of salvation," and "portrayal of salvation."[15] We do not need to pay too close attention to the variations in form. What counts for our consideration is the situation-transforming capacity of the utterance, what Ricoeur would term "redescription."

Thus Lamentations 5:20 ends with a haunting sense of being "forgotten" and "forsaken":

> Why have you *forgotten* us completely?
> Why have you *forsaken* us these many days?

In Isaiah 49:14, the same two terms are reiterated (probably deliberately quoted):

> But Zion said, "The LORD has *forsaken* me,
> my Lord has *forgotten* me." (emphasis added)

But then in 49:15–16, these haunting fearful questions are answered by the God who does not forget or abandon:

> Can a woman *forget* her nursing child,
> or show no compassion for the child of her womb?
> Even these may *forget,*
> yet I will not *forget* you.
> See, I have inscribed you on the palms of my hands;
> your walls are continually before me.
>
> (emphasis added)

Or in Isaiah 54:10, after conceding that there had been a brief abandonment of Israel by God (vv. 7–8) and after comparing the devastation of the exile to the flood in Genesis (v. 9), the poet has God utter a sweeping assurance of God's reliable durability:[16]

15. Claus Westermann, "The Way of the Promise through the Old Testament," in *The Old Testament and Christian Faith: A Theological Discussion,* ed. Bernhard W. Anderson (New York: Harper & Row, 1963), 202–9.

16. On this text, see Walter Brueggemann, "A Shattered Transcendence? Exile and Restoration," in *Problems and Prospects in Biblical Theology,* ed. Ben C. Ollenburger et al. (forthcoming from Abingdon).

> For the mountains may depart
> and the hills be removed,
> but my *steadfast love* shall not depart from you,
> and my *covenant of peace* shall not be removed,
> says the LORD, who has *compassion* on you.
>
> (Isa. 54:10, emphasis added)

This triad of Yahweh's characteristics — steadfast love, covenant of peace, compassion — is more than enough to override the flood, to overcome the absence and shame, and to overmatch the terror of exile.

We are so familiar with such assurances that we may fail to notice what a daring act of faith such an utterance is, how blatantly it speaks against and beyond perceived circumstance, in order to "reconstruct, replace, or redraw the threatened paradigm of meaning." It is an act of powerful faith on the part of the speaker, but also on the part of the listener. The intent of the assurance is to create faith in the listener. The exile was widely seen to be a season of God's absence, and now this poet dares to assert that God is present in that very circumstance, faithfully at work to bring a newness out of the defeat.

The analogue in our own time is for the preacher-poet of the gospel to make such an utterance in the midst of our failed privilege and hegemony. The utterance of assurance is not to prop up the old paradigm, for the assurance comes only after the "representation of the catastrophe," that is, after the felt and expressed situation of lamentation and complaint. The assurance asserts that in the very midst of economic displacement and bewilderment about sexuality, where all old certitudes are in profound jeopardy, just these meanings of a new kind are being wrought by the power and fidelity of God, "new things" shaped like covenantal faithfulness that will become visible only in, with, and through the displacement.[17] Such utterances are indeed "by faith alone." But then, that is always how the gospel is uttered in such problematic circumstance.

---

17. I name economics and sexuality because these are the twin issues that vex and will continue to vex the church. It will be helpful to see that the two are deeply interrelated, as the parallel criticisms of Marx and Freud make clear.

Doxologies of Defiance

The counterpole to lamentation and complaint is the hymn of praise, which emerges from "victory songs." That is, hymns are sung when situations of great trouble are transformed by the power and mercy of God. Israel has been singing such songs since the deliverance from Egypt (Exod. 15:1–18, 21). These daring doxologies sing what Israel has seen and heard about the decisive power and reliable commitment of Yahweh to intrude in life-giving ways in circumstances of defeat, disorder, and death. Thus the doxology of remembrance in Psalm 74:12–17 reaches all the way back to creation and to God's capacity to order chaos. And the despondent worshiper in Psalm 77:11–20 ponders the remembered exodus. Out of these treasured, concrete memories, Israel's hymns also constitute acts of hope and confidence that what God has done in the past is what God will do in the present and in the future.

In the exile, the doxologies are not primarily acts of remembering God's past "wonders," but they are anticipatory assertions concerning what God is about to do. Israel is summoned to sing a "new song," to sing praise for God's sovereign liberating action that is now about to occur (Isa. 42:10).

In the situation of exile in Babylon, it was "self-evident" that the Babylonian gods had triumphed, that Yahweh had failed, either because of weakness or because of indifference. Either way, the evidence suggested that loyalty to Yahweh no longer worked or was worth practicing because other powers could give more reliable and immediate payoffs.

The poetry of II Isaiah, however, will not accept that "self-evident" reading of reality. The hymns offered by the poet are assertions against the evident, insisting that Yahweh's saving power is at the break of new activity. Israel has concluded that God does not care about Israel:

> Why do you say, O Jacob,
>   and speak, O Israel,
> "My way is hidden from the LORD,
>   and my right is disregarded by my God"?
>   (Isa. 40:27)

The responding hymn of verses 28–31 asserts in wondrous lyric that Yahweh is the God of all generations (past, present, future), is not weary or faint or powerless, but gives power to those who hope. The outcome is not only a statement about God but an assurance to those who trust this God:

> Those who wait for the LORD shall renew their strength,
> they shall mount up with wings like eagles,
> they shall run and not be weary,
> they shall walk and not faint. (Isa. 40:31)

Notice that the doxology completely rejects the notion of the rule of the Babylonian gods. Against their apparent rule, it is, so the hymn asserts, in fact Yahweh who holds power and who gives power (cf. 46:1–4).

That same contrast is evident in the defiant doxology of Isaiah 41:21–29. Negatively the gods of Babylon are called to give account of themselves, and they fail miserably (vv. 21–23). This leads to the conclusion that they are nothing, nothing at all. Moreover, those who trust such "nothing gods" are as "nothing" as their gods:

> You, indeed, are nothing
> and your work is nothing at all;
> whoever chooses you is an abomination.
> (Isa. 41:24)

Positively, it is Yahweh who is able to act visibly, decisively, and transformatively (vv. 25–27). Israel's doxologies are characteristically against the data, inviting Israel to live in a "redescribed world," in which meaning has been "reconstructed, replaced, or redrawn."

In our own situation, the hymnic act of praise has become largely innocuous. It happens often among us that praise is either escapist fantasy, or it is a bland affirmation of the status quo. In fact, doxology is a daring political, polemical act that serves to dismiss certain loyalties and to embrace and legitimate other loyalties and other shapes of reality.[18]

---

18. See Walter Brueggemann, "Praise and the Psalms: A Politics of Glad Abandonment," parts 1 and 2, *The Hymn: A Journal of Congregational Song* 43, no. 3 (July 1992): 14–19; no. 4 (October 1992): 14–18.

In the context of II Isaiah, the hymnic wager is on Yahweh's intention for homecoming. Israel in exile refuses the Babylonian gods who
seek to define the world in noncovenantal ways. In our situation of
upheaval and confusion, hymns that celebrate the God of the Bible
wager on a covenantal-neighborly world powered by the neighborli-
ness of God and wager against any characterization of the world that
bets on selfishness, greed, fear, abuse, or despair. Our current world
of bewilderment is often described as though everything good is ending, as though the forces of chaos have won. This hymnic tradition
authorizes the church to identify and redescribe this present place as
the arena in which the rule of the creator-liberator God is working
a wondrous newness. Our singing and utterance of such lyric faith
assert that we will not submit to the gods of fear and anticovenantal
power relations. In such a situation as ours, the words and music for
a "new song" are acts of powerful renewal.

Promises

The assurances and hymns upon which we have commented are anticipatory. That is, they look to the resolve of Yahweh to work a newness
that is not yet visible or in hand. Exiles, however, have a way of
speech that is more directly and singularly preoccupied with God's
sure future, namely, oracles of promise. Israel believes that God can
indeed work a newness out of present shambles and that that newness
will more fully embody God's good will for the world. It is cause for
amazement that Israel's most daring and definitional promises were
uttered in exile, that is, precisely when the evidence seems to preclude
such hope. The promises are assertions that God is not a prisoner of
circumstance but that God can call into existence that which does not
exist (cf. Rom. 4:17).

Here I will cite three of the best-known and most powerful of
such exilic promises. In Jeremiah 31:31–34, the promise asserts that
God will work a new covenant with Israel that is aimed at Torah obedience (v. 33) but is rooted in the overriding reality of forgiveness
(v. 34).[19] The dominant assumption about exile in the Old Testament,

---

19. See the helpful discussion of this passage by Norbert Lohfink, *The Covenant Never
Revoked: Biblical Reflections on Christian-Jewish Dialogue* (New York: Paulist, 1991), 45–57.
Lohfink makes clear that the text cannot be interpreted in a Christian, supersessionist way.

propounded especially in the Deuteronomic tradition, is that exile is punishment (2 Kings 17:7–23; see even Isa. 40:2). This promise, in the face of a theology of guilt and punishment, is an assertion that forgiveness will overpower sin, and Israel's primal theological reality is the future-creating graciousness of Yahweh who will "remember their sin no more."[20]

In Ezekiel 37:1–14, the prophet Ezekiel searches for an adequate metaphor for exile and homecoming. The most extreme imagery available is that exile equals death. But from death, there is no hope, for the power of death is strong and decisive. In a radical rhetorical break, however, the prophet dares to assert that by the power of God's spirit, "I [will] open your graves"; that is, "I will place you on your own soil" (vv. 13–14). Exile is not the last word; that is, death is not the last reality. Israel's situation is not hopeless because God's transformative wind (spirit) blows even in the dismay of exile, in order to work a newness toward life.

The poem of Isaiah 65:17–65 (which may be dated slightly after the return from exile in 520 B.C.E.) offers a "portrayal of salvation" in stunning anticipatory fashion. The poet anticipates a new earth and a new Jerusalem characterized by new social relations, new economic possibilities, and new communion with God. Indeed, the poet foresees a complete and concrete inversion of Israel's current situation of hopelessness.

Notice that all of the promises, specific as they are, are cast as God's own speech, the authority for which is found, not in any visible circumstance, but in the trustworthiness of the God who speaks. It is God's own resolve to work a newness that will impinge upon what seems to be a closed, hopeless situation.

Exiles inevitably must reflect upon the power of promise, upon the capacity of God to work a newness against all circumstance.[21] Promise has become nearly an alien category among us. That is partly an intellectual problem for us because our Enlightenment perception of reality does not believe that there can be any newness "from the out-

---

20. On "forgiveness," see especially the exilic text of 1 Kings 8:27–53.

21. On the practice of promise among exiles in order to fight off despair, see Rubem A. Alves, *Tomorrow's Child: Imagination, Creativity, and the Rebirth of Culture* (New York: Harper & Row, 1972), 182–205. Alves writes: "Why is it so important to go on hoping? Because without hope one will be either dissolved in the existing state of things or devoured by insanity" (193).

side" that can enter our fixed world. And partly the loss of promise is a function of our privilege in the world, whereby we do not in fact want newness but only an enhancement and guarantee of our preferred present tense.

As our white, male, Western privilege comes to an end, we are likely to experience that "ending" as a terrible loss that evokes fear and resentment.[22] Evangelical faith, however, dares to identify what is (for some) an alienating circumstance as the matrix for God's newness (for all). Thus evangelical speech functions to locate the hunches and hints and promises which seem impossible to us that God will indeed work in the midst of our frightening bewilderment. But the preacher will work primarily not from visible hints and hunches precisely because hope is "the conviction of things not seen" (Heb. 11:1), a conviction rooted in the trusted character of God.

The Ministry of Language

Speech, or as Mintz terms it, "the ministry of language," is one of the few available resources for exile.[23] Exiles are characteristically stripped of all else, except speech. And what exiles do is to speak their "mother tongue," that is, the speech learned as children from mothers, as a way to maintain identity in a situation that is identity-denying.

In that ancient world of displacement, the Jews treasured speech that was "redescriptive" precisely because it was not derived from or sanctioned by the managers of the exile. It was, rather, derived from older speech practice of the covenanted community and sanctioned by the evangelical *chutzpah* of poets who dared to credit such defiant utterances as complaints and lamentations, assurances, hymns, and promises. These are indeed forms of speech from Israel's "mother tongue."

In the "modernist" church of our time (liberal and conservative), there has been a loss of "mother-speech," partly because of subtle epistemological erosion and partly because we imagine that other forms of speech are more credible and "make more sense." The truth

---

22. My use of the term "end" here as a sense of terrible loss is intended to counter the argument of Francis Fukuyama, *The End of History and the Last Man* (New York: Free Press, 1992). In my judgment his self-serving argument, that is, self-serving for Western capitalism, is a romantic fantasy. He understands the current "end" to be one of triumph.

23. Mintz, *Hurban*, 29.

is, however, that speech other than our own gradually results in the muteness of the church, for we have nothing left to say when we have no way left to say it. Exiles need, first of all and most of all, a place in which to practice liberated speech that does not want or receive the legitimacy of context. I take it that the old "paradigms of meaning" are indeed deeply under threat among us. We can scarcely pretend otherwise. We may learn from our ancestors in faith that in such a context, we must indeed "represent the catastrophe" and then "reconstruct, replace, or redraw" the paradigms of meaning. Both tasks are demanding. It belongs nonetheless to the speakers rooted in this tradition of liberated, defiant, anticipatory speech to take up these tasks. It is in, with, and from such speech that there come "all things new."

3

DUTY AS DELIGHT
AND DESIRE

Preaching Obedience That Is Not Legalism

WALTER BRUEGGEMANN

We may as well concede at the outset that we live, all of us, in a promiscuous, self-indulgent society that prizes autonomy.[1] As a consequence, "obedience" is a tough notion, which we settle mostly either by the vaguest of generalizations or by confining subject matter to those areas already agreed upon.

I

The fearfulness and avoidance of obedience, as conventionally understood among us, has in my judgment two root causes, both of which are alive and powerful, even though not often frontally articulated.

The first dimension of the problem is the Augustinian-Lutheran dichotomy of "grace and law," which runs very deep in Western theology. In his treatment of Paul, Augustine considerably upped the stakes of the issue in his crushing opposition to Pelagius, and Luther solidified that theological claim by boldly inserting the word "alone" in his reading of Paul, thus "grace *alone.*" It is clear that by "law" Luther meant many different things, seemingly focused especially on life apart from the gospel. The result, however, has been a remarkable aversion to "works," as though obedience to the commands of

---

1. Paul R. McHugh, "Psychiatric Misadventures," in *The Best American Essays 1993*, ed. Joseph Epstein (New York: Ticknor & Fields, 1993), 192, helpfully speaks of "cultural antinomianism" and explores its costliness for society. The best series of case studies for this condition is offered by Robert Bellah et al., *Habits of the Heart: Individualism and Commitment in American Life* (Berkeley: University of California Press, 1985).

God, that is, performances of "works," is in and of itself a denial of the gospel. Luther is of course much more subtle and knowing than this, but thus he has been conventionally interpreted. The outcome has been a notion of gospel without demand, a notion that plays well in a "therapeutic" society.

An aspect of this strong dichotomy has been a latent but pervasive anti-Jewish stereotype. Thus "law" is easily assigned to the "Jews," and the Old Testament becomes a book of commandments that has been superseded by the free gospel of Christ. Such a common maneuver of course fails to understand the core dynamic of covenantal faith shared by Jews and Christians and inevitably feeds anti-Semitism.[2]

It is sufficient here simply to observe that such a reading of the gospel of Paul, powerfully reinforced by a sustained German-Lutheran reading of Romans, is at least open to question. Krister Stendahl has proposed that Augustine and Luther have massively misread Paul, who is concerned not with "guilt" but with Jewish-Christian relations in the early church.[3] And E. P. Sanders has contributed greatly to the exposition of Stendahl's proposal, so this governing dichotomy needs to be seriously challenged and reconsidered.[4] The task of such reconsideration is a difficult one, given the force of these old categories.

The second dimension of our problem is the Enlightenment notion of unfettered freedom of "Man Come of Age." Indeed, the central program of the Enlightenment has been to slough off any larger authority to which obedience is owed, and that with special reference to the traditional authority of the church.[5] This notion of freedom is already rooted in Descartes's establishment of the *human* doubter as the norm of truth. Locke contributed to the cause with his notion of the human person as a rational, free decider, and Kant completed the "Turn toward the Subject" in making the human autonomous ac-

---

2. Paul M. van Buren, *A Christian Theology of the People Israel,* A Theology of the Jewish-Christian Reality 2 (San Francisco: Harper & Row, 1987), 158–59 and passim, has explored a healthier understanding of the matter of torah shared by Christians and Jews.

3. Krister Stendahl, "The Apostle Paul and the Introspective Conscience of the West," *Paul among Jews and Gentiles and Other Essays* (Philadelphia: Fortress, 1976), 78–96.

4. Among his important works on the subject, see E. P. Sanders, *Paul and Palestinian Judaism: A Comparison of Patterns of Religion* (Philadelphia: Fortress, 1977). See his several discussions of "covenantal nomism."

5. For a classic discussion of the issues of the Enlightenment vis-à-vis the traditional authority of the church, see Paul Hazard, *The European Mind 1680–1715* (New York: World Publishing, 1963).

tor the one who will shape functional reality. This Enlightenment ideology has received its popular form in a Freudian theory of repression in which human maturation is the process of emancipation from communal authority, which is extrinsic to the individual person and therefore fundamentally alien to mature humanness. Thus the human goal is movement beyond any restraints that come under the category of repression.

It turns out, of course, that such a model of unfettered freedom is an unreachable mirage. The individual person is never so context-less, and in the end the fantasy of such freedom has culminated in the most choking of conformities.[6] There is, to be sure, an element of truth in Enlightenment models of liberation, but such a notion is almost always insufficiently dialectical to bear upon the actual human situation.

These theological-theoretical matters may seem quite remote from the concrete task of "preaching obedience." In my judgment, however, pastor and congregation must engage these powerful (even if hidden) categories and assumptions in critical and knowing ways, in order to face the commands of God honestly. The reason they must be faced is that they are concretely powerful, even if mostly unarticulated. It is false to take the law/grace dichotomy at face value, as though the Creator of heaven and earth has no overriding, nonnegotiable intention for God's creatures. It is equally false to accept the phony freedom of autonomy and find ourselves more deeply enmeshed in the commands of death. Only the exposure of these false articulations can permit the community of the gospel to discern and accept its true position before God, who loves, delivers, summons, and commands.[7]

II

A rereading of the gospel of grace and a reconsideration of Enlightenment ideology, in my judgment, will lead to a stunning and

6. On the production of conformity and homogeneity by the Enlightenment, see Colin Gunton, *Enlightenment and Alienation: An Essay towards a Trinitarian Theology* (Grand Rapids: Eerdmans, 1985); and his more recent work, *The One, the Three, and the Many: God, Creation, and the Culture of Modernity* (Cambridge: Cambridge University Press, 1993).

7. Emil Fackenheim's *God's Presence in History* (New York: New York University Press, 1970) has shown how the dialectic of "saving and commanding" asserts the primal work of God with Israel.

compelling fresh awareness: our most serious relationships, including our relationship to the God of the gospel, are, at the same time, *profoundly unconditional* and *massively conditional.* One can, I submit, test this odd claim both in terms of our normative theological materials and in terms of our lived experience. Such a notion of course violates all of our either/or Aristotelian logic, but our most treasured relations are not subject to such an exclusionary logic.

Much Old Testament scholarship (including some of my own) has championed the notion that there are two traditions of covenant in the Old Testament, one unconditional (Abraham and David) and one conditional (Moses).[8] While this is critically correct, our theological task is to try to understand these textual claims taken all together.[9] The evidence to which I am drawn suggests in powerful ways that *conditional/unconditional* and *law/grace* are unworkable categories for understanding our most serious and treasured relationships. And these misguided polarities create great crises for understanding the odd dialectical character of the gospel.

We may take as emblematic of such relationships that are neither conditional nor unconditional, as does the Old Testament texts, the relations of husband-wife and parent-child. In either of these at its best, it is clear that the relationship is unconditional; that is, there is no circumstance under which the relationship will be voided. And yet in these very same relationships, there are high and insistent "expectations" of the other that shade over into demands.[10]

---

8. The clearest, most direct statement of this tension is that of David Noel Freedman, "Divine Commitment and Human Obligation: The Covenant Theme," *Interpretation* 18 (October 1964): 419–31. Jon D. Levenson, *Sinai and Zion: An Entry into the Jewish Bible* (New York: Winston, 1985), has written a programmatic rebuttal of the antithesis commonly assumed in scholarship.

9. See the exposition of Brevard S. Childs, *Biblical Theology of the Old and New Testaments: Theological Reflection on the Christian Bible* (Minneapolis: Fortress, 1992), 532–65; and *Old Testament Theology in a Canonical Context* (Philadelphia: Fortress, 1985), 51–83.

10. Dennis H. Wrong, *The Problem of Order: What Unites and Divides Society* (New York: Free Press, 1994), 42–58, has written suggestively about the authority of expectation, though he is concerned for political theory and not theological force. He writes:

> The ambiguity of expectation becomes apparent only when we consider its use in communications such as that of a mother telling her child that she "expects" obedience at school to the teacher, or of the admiral addressing the fleet who affirms that "England expects every man to do his duty."
> The mother and the admiral are not simply predicting out loud future events or common interest . . . their utterances to the child and to the assembled fleet are in the imperative mode: the expectations asserted are intended to bring about the conduct they claim to be anticipating. . . . The child, after all, knows, and the mother knows the

And when these expectations are not met, there may be wounded-ness, alienation, or even rejection, even though the wounded party is powerfully committed.[11] The truth is that there is something inscrutable about such relationships that are both conditional or un-conditional or, perhaps we should say, neither unconditional nor conditional. If we seek to make one term or the other final in charac-terizing such a relationship, we destroy the inscrutability that belongs to and defines the relationship.[12]

It may indeed be regarded as a far leap from our experience with such relationships as husband-wife and parent-child to our relation with God. It is of course a leap made artistically and boldly in the text itself. It will, moreover, be objected that one cannot reason by analogy or metaphor about God, and yet it is the only language we have for this most serious and freighted of all relationships. Moreover, we must ask why the poets of ancient Israel chose to speak this way about God. I suggest that such images are utilized because the poets who have given us our primal language for God are seeking a way to voice an inscrutability that overrides our logic and is more like the inscrutability of serious relationships than it is like anything else.[13]

The covenant God has with us, with Israel, with the world, is a command-premised relation. The covenant is based in command, and God expects to be obeyed.[14] There are, moreover, sanctions and con-sequences of disobedience that cannot be avoided, even as there are

---

child knows, that disobedience at school will be reported at home and lead to possibly unpleasant results....

Expectations may, I have argued, function as imperatives, as normative demands con-straining the human objects of expectation to conform to them.... The emergence of expectations-cum-norms out of recurrent interaction is a process that goes on all the time, if often in trivial and evanescent ways. (pp. 42–43, 46, 51)

11. Notice that often the "sanction" is not articulated but is inherent in the expectation itself because of the authority of the one who expects.

12. This seems to be recognized even in popular ways, so the attempt at "unconditional" finally requires some conditionality. See the belated discovery of this in William H. Masters and Virginia E. Johnson, *The Pleasure Bond: A New Look at Sexuality and Commitment* (Boston: Brown and Little, 1974), and the analysis of Daniel Yankelovich, *New Rules: Searching for Self-Fulfillment in a World Turned Upside Down* (New York: Bantam, 1982).

13. This is a point at which Karl Barth's resistance of the *analogia entis* and his embrace of *analogia fidei* might be considered. Eberhard Busch, *Karl Barth: His Life from Letters and Autobiographical Texts* (Philadelphia: Fortress, 1976), 215–16 and passim, places Barth's concerns in context.

14. E. Kutsch, "Gesetz und Gnade. Probleme des alttestamentlichen Bundesbegriffs," *Zeitschrift für die alttestamentliche Wissenschaft* 79 (1967): 18–35, goes so far as to suggest that "covenant" (*berith*) in fact means "obligation."

gifts and joys along with obedience.[15] The torah is given for guidance so that Israel (and all of Israel's belated heirs) are "clued in" to the defining expectations of this relationship. The torah makes clear that the holy "Other" in this relationship is an agent with will and purpose that must be taken seriously and cannot be disregarded or mocked.

Thus it is a *covenantal relation* that is the "underneath category" to which "grace and law," "conditional and unconditional," are subsets.[16] The Other in this relation is a real, live Other who initiates, shapes, watches over, and cares about the relation. The Other is both *mutual* with us and *incommensurate* with us, in a way not unlike a parent is mutual and incommensurate with a child or a teacher is mutual and incommensurate with a student. This means that the relation is endlessly open, alive, giving and demanding, and at risk. This Holy Other may on occasion act in stunning mutuality, being with and for the second party, and so draw close in mercy and compassion, in suffering and forgiveness. It is, however, this same God who may exhibit God's self in unaccommodating incommensurability with rigorous expectation and dreadfulness, when expectations are not met. It is our desperate effort to reduce or "solve" the wonder of "the Holy one in our midst" that leads to such distortions as law and grace, freedom and servitude, unconditional and conditional.[17] No such pairing can adequately contain the inscrutability, liveliness, danger, and unsettled quality of this relationship. Israel thus knows that torah is *guidance,* in order to be joyously "on the way," a way that constitutes the well-being of the relationship.[18]

III

This core insight about the richness of a covenantal relation still leaves for the preacher and the congregation the demanding work of tak-

---

15. George E. Mendenhall, *Law and Covenant in Israel and the Ancient Near East* (Pittsburgh: Biblical Colloquium, 1955), made the case that "sanctions" belong to the structure and substance of covenant. More generally see the discussion of Wrong (n. 10) on the reality of sanctions in social relations.

16. "Covenantal nomism" (on which see Sanders, n. 4) nicely juxtaposes terms that articulate the subtle dimensions of covenant as a *relation* and as a *demand*.

17. On this phrase, see the old but reliable discussion of Walther Eichrodt, "The Holy One in Your Midst: The Theology of Hosea," *Interpretation* 15 (July 1961): 259–73.

18. On "the way" as a governing image for Israel's life of obedient faith, see James Muilenburg, *The Way of Israel: Biblical Faith and Ethics* (New York: Harper & Brothers, 1961); and Paul M. Van Buren, *Discerning the Way,* A Theology of the Jewish Christian Reality (New York: Seabury, 1980).

ing seriously the specific commands of this covenantal Other. Clearly
the commands and guidance of the God of Israel and of the church
are not vague and fuzzy, but quite concrete in how they concern the
specificities of life. Those bound with this God are summoned to
act differently in every sphere of life. Indeed, obedience consists in
bringing every zone of our existence under the will, purpose, and expectation of this covenantal partner. While the concrete enactments
of these commands in almost every case face ambiguity and complexity,[19] the most crucial issue for reflection and preaching is to frame
the commands so that they are not alien impositions, extrinsic to our
life, but belong to and are embraced as definitional for the very fabric
of our existence.[20]

For that purpose, I suggest two possible interpretive strategies. The
first is that the commands of God are the *disciplines essential to the
revolution* that is Yahwism.[21] Every serious revolutionary movement
requires exacting disciplines of its adherents. And while the requirements may vary, they all in substance concern single-minded devotion
to the revolution, without any doubt, ambiguity, or reservation. A
revolution has no chance of success unless all of its adherents are singularly committed to the vision and the project and are willing to play
their assigned role with unquestioning reliability and responsiveness.

The revolution to which the biblical community is summoned is to
enact in the world of social affairs a new practice of social relationships marked by justice, mercy, and peace, which touches all of life. In
order to engage in such a practice, all those committed to this revolutionary vision are expected to enact the daily requirements concerning
self toward God, and self toward neighbor, in order to "advance the
revolution."

---

19. Concerning the ambiguity and complexity of the commandments, which require on-
going interpretation, see Walter Brueggemann, "The Commandments and Liberated, Liberating
Bonding," *Interpretation and Obedience: From Faithful Reading to Faithful Living* (Minneapolis:
Fortress, 1991), 145–58.

20. I understand legalism to refer to commands that are imposed but not gladly received and
embraced as one's own. The model of Job's friends is the standard example in the Bible. Such
imposition tends to be rigid and coercive, without taking into account the impact of context
or experience. On this matter as it relates to freedom and health, see Christopher Bollas, *The
Shadow of the Object: Psychoanalysis of the Unthought Known* (New York: Columbia University
Press, 1987), 135–56, and his notion of a "normatic personality."

21. More than anyone else, Norman Gottwald, *The Tribes of Yahweh: A Sociology of the Religion of Liberated Israel, 1250–1050 B.C.* (Maryknoll, N.Y.: Orbis, 1979), 489–92 and passim,
has shown the ways in which Israel is revolutionary in terms of its social intention. Gottwald's
articulation is enormously valuable, even if one does not follow all of his sociohistorical analysis.

Or to change the figure slightly, Jesus and his disciples, that is, the ones under his discipline, are "on the way" as the "kingdom of God draws near," a kingdom in which the "normalcies" of life are turned on their head. The disciples are variously summoned and dispatched to order their life around "prayer and fasting," around empty-handed healing power, to live their lives as concrete testimony that the new realm is "at hand" and can be lived and practiced here and now.

In order to make this approach to obedience convincing, believers must come to see their baptism as entry into a new vision of reality, which carries with it all sorts of new possibilities that the world thinks impossible.[22] This vision of reality is an oddity in the world, at odds with all the conventional orderings of society — political, economic, and social. This "signing on" is not an "extra" added to a normal life but entails a reordering of all of one's life from the ground up. The specificities of obedience must constantly be seen as derivative from and in the service of the larger revolution. It is clear that Moses imagined a whole new way of being in the world, a way ordered as covenant, and the commands of Sinai provide the guidance for that new way. And in like fashion, it is clear that the movement around Jesus evoked such hostility and resistance precisely because his movement subverted all conventional practices and forms in the world. No doubt such demands and disciplines became "legalistic" when the concrete requirement was no longer understood to derive from a larger revolutionary intention.

I am aware that such a notion of "revolutionary discipline" will not be easily compelling for most of us in excessively complacent establishment Christianity. I do imagine, however, that for many persons (especially young people), such a notion may indeed be a powerful attraction, for it is an enactment of a powerful hope for newness midst an increasingly failed and despairing society.

In any case, I suggest a second strategy for "preaching obedience." It is this: believers are those who love God with their whole heart or, more colloquially for Christians, "love the Lord Jesus." Such love is to be understood in all its rich implication, both as *agape* and *eros*, as true heart's desire.[23] This is imagery not often utilized in our Calvinist

---

22. On the relationship between baptism and preaching, see William H. Willimon, *Peculiar Speech: Preaching to the Baptized* (Grand Rapids: Eerdmans, 1992).

23. It will be recognized that my approach here flies in the face of the classic arguments of

inheritance, beset as we are with a heavy sense of duty. But alongside *duty* in any serious relationship are *desire* and *delight*, the energetic will to be with the one loved, to please the one loved, to find in the joy of the one loved one's own true joy. Thus one in love is constantly asking in the most exaggerated way, What else can I do in order to delight the beloved? In such a context, one does not count the cost but anticipates that when the beloved is moved in joy, it will be one's own true joy as well. Indeed, in such a condition, one can find joy only in the joy of the beloved, not apart from the joy of the beloved.

Thus the psalmist can speak of such true heart's desire:

> One thing I asked of the LORD,
>   that I will seek after:
> to live in the house of the LORD
>   all the days of my life,
> to behold the beauty of the LORD,
>   and to inquire in his temple. (Ps. 27:4)

> Whom have I in heaven but you?
>   And there is nothing on earth that I desire other than you.
>   (Ps. 73:25)

Of the last verse, Calvin comments:

> I know that thou by thyself, apart from every other object, art sufficient, yea, more than sufficient for me, and therefore I do not suffer myself to be carried away after a variety of desires, but rest in and am fully contented with thee. In short, that we may be satisfied with God alone, it is of importance for us to know the plenitude of the blessings which he offers for our acceptance.[24]

Anders Nygren, *Agape and Eros* (Philadelphia: Westminster, 1932, 1938, 1939, 1953). I do this with considerable diffidence because I am thoroughly schooled in Nygren's argument. I have come to think, however, that Nygren imposed categories that may have been required in his context, but that in doing so, he overlooked dimensions of the ethic of Israel and the church that moved beyond duty to the embrace of joy in faith. For our purposes, Nygren's discussion of Augustine (pp. 449–563) is especially important.

I should also mention that William Moran, "The Ancient Near Eastern Background of the Love of God in Deuteronomy," *Catholic Biblical Quarterly* 25 (1963): 77–87, has shown that in some cases in the ancient Near East, *love* is a political word bespeaking acknowledgment of sovereignty.

24. John Calvin, *Commentary on the Book of Psalms, Volume 2* (Grand Rapids: Baker, 1979), 155. It should be noted, however, that Calvin still resists the notion of the intrinsic satisfaction

The true believer desires most of all being with the beloved. None has understood this as well or as eloquently as Augustine, who saw that the most elemental craving of our life is communion with God. He begins his *Confessions* with the well-known affirmation: "Thou awakest us to delight in Thy praise; for Thou madest us for Thyself, and our heart is restless, until it repose in Thee."[25] And in his subsequent comment, he adds, "Thou also gavest me to desire no more than Thou gavest."[26] This sense of keen desire, not without its erotic dimension, is echoed in Bach's sterner notion of Jesus as the "joy of man's desiring." Thus obedience is a concrete, visible way of enacting and entering that desire, so that duty converges completely with the desire and delight of communion. It is not that obedience is instrumental and makes communion possible, but obedience itself is a mode of "being with" the desired in joy, delight, and well-being. In a quite concrete way, it is profoundly satisfying to do what the beloved most delights in.

Now I imagine that like "disciplines for revolution," the notion of "the desire of the beloved" will not be easy in the starchier traditions of Christian faith. Our more preferred strategy has been to renounce desire and focus on duty, on the affirmation that desire per se is an

---

of the relationship and must appeal to "the plentitude of blessing" that seem extrinsic to the relation of communion itself.

25. Augustine, *The Confession of St. Augustine, Bishop of Hippo* (New York: E. P. Dutton, 1951), 1.

26. Ibid., 5. Special attention should be given to the recent study of the *Confessions* by Margaret R. Miles, *Desire and Delight: A New Reading of Augustine's Confessions* (New York: Crossroad, 1992). Against the grain of the argument of Nygren, Miles proposes that the *Confessions* are intended by Augustine to be a "text of pleasure" and that the pleasure of the reader is linked to Augustine's own struggle for pleasure. Augustine's argument is that he tried every pleasure the world could offer and only finds his true desire in communion with God. This is not a stifling of desire but the proper focus on the desire that is appropriate to the human heart. Miles summarizes her argument:

The *Confessions* is, among other things, a narrative deconstruction of what is ordinarily thought of as pleasurable, and a reconstruction of "true" pleasure.... He was quite clear about what constituted the condition of greatest pleasure by the time he wrote the *Confessions* (20).... The pleasure experiment had come to a dead end (32).... The key to pleasure, for Augustine, was ideally not the sacrifice of some pleasures so that others could be cultivated. It was the ordering of all the pleasures of a human life so that those associated with enjoyment of objects in the sensible world would not usurp all of a person's attention and affection. When pleasures are constellated around a single object of love, he said, they can be enjoyed without fear of distraction (37).... Augustine learned more than he acknowledged from sex, that he learned "the deep and irreplaceable knowledge of [his] capacity for joy" from his sexual experience, and that it was precisely *this* experimental knowledge from which Augustine extrapolated his model of spiritual pleasure (pp. 20, 32, 37, 71).

ignoble enterprise. This way of understanding obedience in relation to desire, however, honors the reality that we are indeed desiring creatures. God has made us so, and so we are. The work of obedience then is not to squelch desire or deny it, as some modes of piety are wont to do, for then denied desire breaks out in destructive ways. Our work rather is to critique distorted desire and refocus desire on the true and faithful subject of our proper delight and longing. The intention of consumerism and its ideology of advertising is to distort and misdirect desire, as though the foundational desire of our life is for shoes, deodorant, beer, a car, or the best detergent. At the core of our creatureliness, however, such desires are fundamentally irrelevant. That is not what we want of life, and they do not satisfy.

Faith confesses that it is none other than the very Creator of heaven and earth who constitutes our true desire, so that only when our hearts rest in God can our restlessness be ended and satisfied. Thus the Commandments are specific strategies for redirecting and reaffirming legitimate desire, not in any way a denial of desire, but in full affirmation of true desire. Thus God is the one for whom we seek, "as a deer longs for flowing streams" (Ps. 42:1). The metaphor suggests, according to the older translations, that the faithful "pant for" God and must have God for the wholeness of life. It is no wonder that obedience is a joy and delight because it is an act in and of itself of communion with the one for whom we constantly and rightly yearn.

IV

The core summons to obedience, that is, (*a*) the core disciplines for the revolution and (*b*) the core practices of our true desire, are voiced in the Decalogue.[27] As is well known, the two "tablets" of the ten commands are focused on love of God and love of neighbor. On these two enterprises "hang all the torah and the prophets" (Matt. 22:40). Such a simple prospectus for obedience comprehends enormous teaching material through which to invite the baptized to a new life of *revolutionary devotion* and *singleness of desire*.

---

27. On the Decalogue, see Walter Harrelson, *The Ten Commandments and Human Rights*, Overtures to Biblical Theology (Philadelphia: Fortress, 1980); and Childs, *Old Testament Theology*, 63–83.

The first four commands concerning the love of God reflect on the true subject of our life, the holy God who is our alpha and omega, the source and goal of all our life. This is the baseline for all biblical preaching and the primal claim of our faith. Our life consists in loving God for God's own sake. That is what we are created to do.[28]

How odd to yearn toward God! The commands in Exodus 20:1–7 assert that the primal quality and character of Yahweh deabsolutize every other claim and loyalty and invite the renunciation of every addictive loyalty, conservative or liberal, which drives our life toward restlessness and phoniness. Moreover, the commands show that God is an "end" and not a "means," has no utilitarian value, but is to be loved purely for God's own sake. Such an affirmation about God cuts against all calculating obedience. Long before Job, Moses understood that Israel is called to "serve God for nought" (Job 1:9), that is, to gain nothing but only to be in this lively relation of duty and delight. Imagine what would happen if the church talked honestly about deabsolutizing all our quarrelsome addictions of mind and heart, which tend to make all sorts of things absolutes that draw our life into knotted stomachs, clenched fists, and stern speech![29]

The second tablet (Exod. 20:8–17) asserts that the second true desire of our life, derivative from the first, is to have "good neighbors," that is, to live in a neighborhood. A true neighborhood is never a gift that floats down from the sky but is wrought through the revolutionary work of obedience.[30] If we ever gain clarity about our true desire, it will quickly become evident to us that the yearning for good neighbors cannot be satisfied by any shoes, deodorant, beer, car, or detergent. They are not what we desire! And so our energy might be redirected toward neighborly matters like housing, education, health care and away from coveting (Exod. 20:17) and all the distortions of commandments five through nine that serve coveting

---

28. This is of course reminiscent of the classic answer of the Westminster Catechism, "Man's Chief Concern is to glorify God and enjoy him forever." It is striking that the second half of the sentence speaks of the "enjoyment of God," which is the satisfaction of desire that encompasses duty and moves beyond duty to delight.

29. A proviso is important — such a notion is not an invitation for the preacher to focus on his or her favorite causes or animosities. My impression is that rightly done the notion of critical obedience gives aid and comfort to no one but challenges all of our pet modes of utilitarian obedience.

30. On this theme, see Gerhard von Rad, "Brother and Neighbor in the Old Testament," *God at Work in Israel* (Nashville: Abingdon, 1980), 183–93.

(Exod. 20:8–16). It is no wonder that the Decalogue is at the center
of the Reformation catechisms and that Luther and Calvin spent so
much energy on them. Note well that when revolutionary vision and
true desire are manifested, it becomes exceedingly difficult to be coercive and scolding about obedience. These commands are not primarily
social restraints or modes of social control but are about possibilities
for life that emerge from "coming down where we ought to be." But
conversely, when we have become ambivalent about the requirements
of the revolution or caught in distorted desires, it is predictable that
what begins as an offer of communion becomes coerciveness. And yet
it is clear no amount of reproof can help people find their way into
true communion by way of revolutionary passion or focused desire.
Such passion and desire are not generated by strident insistence or
ideological imposition.

V

It is only slightly reductive to say that the two great accents of Freud
and Marx, sexuality and economics, are the two great arenas for evangelical obedience and the two zones in which we decide about our
devotion to the covenantal revolution and where we enact our true
desire. It follows that sexuality and economics, zones of great power,
are also the most likely candidates for distortion and loss of the very
communion for which we so yearn.

Freud understood that sexuality is a sphere of endless inscrutability,
the arena of our true selves and the place in our life for deepest deception and pathology. Thus obedience in sexuality is a primary agenda
of evangelical faith, as is evident by the enormously destructive quar-
rels and high investment of energy in the church, after long centuries
of repression, domination, and exploitation.

It is relatively easy (and I think useless) for the church simply to
champion a flat "sex ethic" of a quite traditional kind. That of course
is one very live option in the church.[31] But if obedience in sexuality is
to reflect and derive from (either or both) discipline for the revolution

---

31. Marva J. Dawn, *Sexual Character: Beyond Technique to Intimacy* (Grand Rapids: Eerdmans, 1993), has shown in a fine study how a rather conventional sexual ethic is open to a much
more dense significance.

and/or a core desire for communion, then the categories of covenantal fidelity and covenantal freedom must be primary ingredients in our thinking and acting. Such a perspective requires much more than embracing traditional mores because fidelity means something quite different from "abstaining" or "staying married" or "being straight." It means rather being in a relation that is genuinely life-giving and life-receiving, where the work of neighbor regard is practiced. And covenantal freedom means finding modes of fidelity congruent with one's true self and the capacity to be emancipated from "legal" relationships that are in fact destructive and hopelessly demeaning. Thus the specificity of obedience in sexuality may most often come down to a "set of workable conventions," but when that set of conventions is deeply coercive, it does not serve the covenantal revolution, and instead of focusing true desire, it likely crushes desire or misdirects it, so that one's true self is cut off from God and neighbor.[32]

Marx understood, conversely, that money is a sphere of endless inscrutability, an arena of our true selves, and a place in our life for deep deception and alienation. Obedience with money is a powerful agenda for evangelical faith, as is evident by the profound disagreements in the church about ways in which to think about the earning, saving, investing, sharing, and spending of money and the relative merits of different economic systems and policies. The Bible, moreover, spends enormous amounts of space and energy on such issues.

It is relatively easy (and I think unhelpful) for the church to champion a traditional ethics of money that simply reflects the practices of society, whether in a market economy or a state economy. It is usual practice for the church in our U.S. context to embrace what is conventionally understood as "Protestant work ethic." It turns out, however, that such a work ethic is for our time and place inordinately simplistic and fails to take into account the ambiguities and complexities of a global economic reality with astonishing disparities between "haves" and "have-nots."[33] Moreover, such an ethic does not seem to make enough contact with those who are so affluent that they

---

32. It cannot be said too often that after Israel (or we) arrive at workable rules, the rules endlessly require ongoing interpretation to take account of context, experience, and new learning. This is inevitable, and we either do it knowingly or without recognizing that we are doing such interpretation.

33. See the thoughtful discussion of the issues by Ulrich Duchrow, *Global Economy: A Confessional Issue for the Churches?* (Geneva: WCC Publications, 1987).

can create smaller zones of well-being that screen out the presence of the neighbor.[34] It seems increasingly clear that the culminating command of Moses, "Thou shalt not covet," now requires a carefully nuanced exposition that for affluent people moves well beyond such conventions as a "tithe" and addresses the systemically driven acquisitiveness of a consumer ethic in which neighbor questions have evaporated.[35]

As in sexuality, so in economics, covenantal obedience concerns the practice of covenantal fidelity and covenantal freedom, fidelity to see that all of our resources are held in trust in and for the neighbor with whom life is shared and freedom that entails the practice of choices that attend both to the genuine regard of self and the genuine delight in generosity, which enhances the neighborhood. True covenantal desire is not satisfied by acquisitiveness, even on a grand scale, but is satisfied only by the valuing of neighbor, even as self is valued. A reordered perception of obedience in economics is of enormous urgency for the covenantal revolution. It entails a repentance from false desire to which we have become blindly and uncritically committed.

It will be helpful, and in the end necessary, to see that obedience in sexuality and obedience in economics are of a piece. The interrelatedness of the two spheres of obedience exposes a profound contradiction in our common life in the United States. It is conventional among us (and echoed by the more conservative voices of the church) to seek to impose puritanical restraint upon sexuality, all the while encouraging economic promiscuity for the sake of "economic growth."[36] It is not, however, a gain to reverse the process (with dissenting liberals in the church) to encourage economic transformation while being uncritically and thoughtlessly more open about liberty in sexuality. Either way, such disparity sends mixed signals and fails to maintain the del-

---

34. John Kenneth Galbraith, *The Culture of Contentment* (Boston: Houghton Mifflin, 1992), has written an acute study of this propensity in enclaves of wealth in our society.

35. Marvin Chaney, "You Shall Not Covet Your Neighbor's House," *Pacific Theological Review* 15 (winter 1982): 3–13, has shown how the tenth commandment is concerned with policies and practices of systemic acquisitiveness.

36. A classic example of this incongruity is the way in which Roman Catholics in this country are uncompromisingly zealous about the issue of abortion (and other matters of sexuality) but are largely indifferent to the wondrous Bishops' Letter on economics. Roman Catholics are no more caught in this than other Christians. I cite the example only because the Pastoral Letters of the bishops would make possible a discussion of both issues, but that discussion is almost everywhere resisted.

icacy of fidelity and freedom that belongs to covenantal relations.[37]
Both coercive restraint and sanctioned promiscuity, whether in sexuality or in economics, violate the profound relatedness that belongs
to evangelical obedience. It is clear, in my judgment, that the church
must learn to speak differently about both spheres, in relation to each
other and in relation to the larger issues of genuine revolution and
true desire.

VI

It is my judgment that we live in a moment in the U.S. church that
requires a serious and explicit rethinking of the meaning of faithful obedience. At the core of evangelical faith is the claim that faith
knows some things that matter for genuine life, which are now urgent
for our society. Such an explicit rethinking, which is the work of the
whole congregation, may operate with these affirmations:

1. The Enlightenment offer of unfettered freedom without accountability is an unreachable mirage, an illusion never available to us.

2. The neat and conventional antithesis between law and grace
   is a distortion of faith because there are no unconditional or
   conditional relationships in the gospel, but only relationships
   of fidelity that prize both freedom and accountability, the two
   always intertwined and to be negotiated.

3. Baptism is induction into the revolution of the coming rule of
   God. Like every revolution, this one has demanding disciplines
   that distinguish its adherents from all others.

4. Baptism is an acknowledgement of our true desire, our eagerness
   to be with, commune with, delight in, and delight through glad
   obedience to this life-giving Holy Other.

5. It is precisely in our most primary zones of sexuality and economics that the demands and desires of this alternative life

---

37. This contradiction especially sends mixed messages to children and young people. As the
commoditization of all of life is encouraged, it is difficult then to imagine that sexuality is an
exception to the general rule of promiscuity on which our consumer society is dependent.

are most demanding and most satisfying. Those demands and desires consist, not in the voiced demands of conventional morality nor in the self-indulgence that is an alternative to the flat demand, but in the struggle for the interface of freedom and faithfulness, which requires endless interpretive work and reflection.

6. Rejection of disciplines of the revolution and the distortion of our true desire may take place either through flat, one-dimensional traditionalism or through self-indulgence. Such rejection and distortion constitute a betrayal of baptism and an attempt to live at least some of our life outside this coming rule, and according to the rules of the kingdom of death.

7. Willingness to join the revolution or to practice this core desire can never be coerced. Such engagement is possible only by those who perceive their true identity in this coming rule. And then the disciplines and desire are winsome, joyous, and life-giving, not at all burdensome.

VII

In the core Mosaic proclamation of Deuteronomy 6:5–6, immediately following the summons that Israel should listen (*shema*), Israel is told:

> You shall love the LORD your God with all your heart, and with all your soul, and with all your might. Keep these words that I am commanding you today in your heart.

Moses nicely juxtaposes *love* and *keep commandments* because doing the will of the beloved is the way we enact love. Moreover, commandments are to be kept "in your heart"; that is, they are not extrinsic, imposed, or coerced, but inhaled and embraced as one's own true will and intention.

This core summons is fleshed out in Deuteronomy 13:4:

> The LORD your God you shall follow, him alone you shall fear, his commandments you shall keep, his voice you shall hear (*shema*), him you shall serve, and to him you shall hold fast.

In this series of imperative verbs of obedience, two matters may be noticed. First, in Hebrew in this English translation, the word order is inverted to give emphasis to the object of the verbs, "him ... him ... him ... him." It is like a lover saying, "You, you, you."[38]

Second, the last phrase, which the NRSV renders "hold fast" (*dbk*), is elsewhere "cleve" as in Genesis 2:24. It is a term of deep loyalty and devotion, a kind of personal, passionate attachment that far outruns any external, extrinsic rule. Moses envisions a relation of affectionate trust.

Finally, in Mark 10:17–22, Jesus does "pastoral care" for a person who seeks for "meaning" in his life. Jew that he is, Jesus responds to the man by asserting that the assurance he is seeking is found in full obedience to Israel's core commandments. Jesus assumes the man already knows the Commandments. Beyond the commands, Jesus moves to "second level" obedience: "Go, sell what you own, and give the money to the poor, ... come, follow me." It is as though the Commandments are elemental, "first level" access to the revolution, but serious pastoral care moves to a more radical reorientation of life.

We observe three items in this narrative:

1. Jesus does not impose the Commandments upon the man. The commands are not Jesus' idea. They are already there and already known at the beginning of the exchange. They are a premise of the conversation, to which Jesus can make appeal. Jesus credits the man with knowing them, so there is not a cubit of coercion in the response Jesus makes to the man's serious inquiry. Nonetheless, the response of Jesus is indeed a serious one. A good future is to be shaped by what is known of who God is and what God desires.

---

38. Martin Buber, *Tales of the Hasadim: The Early Masters* (London: Thames & Hudson, 1956), 212, cites such a prayer from the rabbi of Berditchev:

> Where I wander — You!
> Where I ponder — You!
> Only you, You again, always You!
> You! You! You!
> When I am gladdened — You!
> When I am saddened — You!
> Only You, You again, always You!
> You! You! You! ...

2. Jesus loved the man (v. 21). Good pastoral care depends upon such a positive disposition toward the subject. Such love, however, does not lead to the romantic easiness of unconditional acceptance. It leads rather to truth telling, which concerns obedience — nothing imposed, nothing harsh, nothing quarrelsome, only uncompromising truth telling about the shape of well-being, spoken in love.

3. Jesus' love, plus the assumption of the Commandments, leads to a startling new demand, a demand too heavy for the questioner. The man decided not to join the revolution and decided to hold to his other "desire" of great possessions.

There is no anger or scolding in this meeting. We are not told that Jesus loved him any the less for his decision. But Jesus' love toward him, like that of Moses, is obedience shaped. Jesus was clearly not much committed to "membership growth" in his little flock under revolutionary discipline. The difficulty of course is that truth telling about well-being in a promiscuous society declares our common desires to be deathly. Obedience thus takes the form of alternative desire. When the Holy One is supremely desired, is the "joy of loving hearts," obedience becomes joy, and duty becomes delight. Such a claim is difficult in the midst of misperceived Enlightenment freedom and in distorted "free grace." But that in itself is no reason to doubt its life-giving truth.

Israel knew that obedience is the path to genuine life. The commands are a mode of God's grace:

> The law of the LORD is perfect,
>   reviving the soul;
> the decrees of the LORD are sure,
>   making wise the simple;
> the precepts of the LORD are right,
>   rejoicing the heart;
> the commandment of the LORD is clear,
>   enlightening the eyes;
> the fear of the LORD is pure,
>   enduring forever;

the ordinances of the LORD are true
and righteous altogether.
More to be desired are they than gold,[39]
even much fine gold;
sweeter also than honey,
and drippings of the honeycomb. (Ps. 19:7–10)

---

39. It is worth noticing that the term "desired" is *hmd*, the same word that is rendered "covet" in the commandment. Israel properly covets, that is, desires the Commandments, the same desiring done by the couple in the garden in Genesis. Israel is supposed to "desire." It matters decisively *what* Israel desires.

4

PRACTICE PREACHING

Stanley M. Hauerwas

Can (or Should) We Practice Preaching?

"Practice preaching?" What could that mean? To practice preaching seems as odd as the suggestion that someone might "practice homosexuality." How in the world would you practice being a homosexual? I understand how you might practice baseball, but how can you practice homosexuality?[1] Is preaching closer to baseball than being a homosexual? I think preaching is closer to baseball than homosexuality, but why will take some explaining.

Ken Woodward, in an article in *Commonweal*, "Ushering in the Age of the Laity: Some Cranky Reservations," observed, "When journalistic colleagues discover that I am a Roman Catholic they always ask, 'Are you practicing?' to which I invariably reply: 'I stopped practicing a long time ago,' which is to say, I just go out and do it."[2] Surely

---

1. Actually, "practicing homosexuality" is not as odd as it may sound. I suspect homosexual relations are no less complex than any human relation. To be sustained they require a great deal of practice. Marriage names that institution for Christians through which we are given the time to develop practices we name as love. That same-sex relations are denied that institution make such relations all the harder.

2. Ken Woodward, "Ushering in the Age of the Laity: Some Cranky Reservations," *Commonweal* 121, no. 15 (September 9, 1994): 9. Woodward goes on to observe,

> What is it about Roman Catholicism, I've often wondered, that takes so much practice? I mean, it's not like learning to play the piano. Why is it you never hear of a practicing Presbyterian? Or a practicing Pentecostal? "Observant" won't do either, as in the sentence, "He's an observant Jew." I know lots of practicing Catholics who are not terribly observant. "Born again" simply doesn't fit Catholics, implying as it does that one has been "saved" through accepting Jesus as his "personal Lord and Savior." Now I think we all need to be converted — over and over again, but having a personal savior has always struck me as, well, elitist, like having a personal tailor. I'm satisfied to have the same Lord and Savior as everyone else. Besides, Catholics can never be certain they are saved, even if they went to Notre Dame, which is one of the reasons Catholicism is so interesting.

For my reflections on why Catholics might be asked whether they are "practicing," see my "A Homage to Mary and to the University Called Notre Dame," *South Atlantic Quarterly* 93, no. 3 (summer 1994): 717–26.

preaching is like being a Roman Catholic. That is, you just go out and do it. So to suggest that one should practice preaching does not seem quite right.

I have argued, however, that being a Christian is very much like learning how to be a practitioner of a craft. For example, in *After Christendom*, I suggested that we ought to think of making disciples the way a bricklayer is trained.[3] I did so to emphasize that Christianity is not so much a set of beliefs that are meant to give our lives meaning, but rather to be a Christian is to be initiated into a community with skills, not unlike learning to lay brick, that are meant to transform our lives. To be initiated into a craft requires, of course, apprenticeship to a master through which we learn the basic habits of the craft sufficient for us to practice the craft as well as to discover the innovations necessary for the craft to have a future.

The notion of craft and the skills essential to the craft are natural to me, of course, as someone who has emphasized the importance of the virtues as the way to display the nature of the Christian moral life. The virtues, as Alasdair MacIntyre reminds us, are correlative to the notion of practice. By *practice*, MacIntyre means "any coherent and complex form of socially established, cooperative human activity through which goods internal to that form of activity are realized in the course of trying to achieve those standards of excellence which are appropriate to, and partially definitive of, that form of activity, with the result that human powers to achieve excellence, and human conceptions of the ends and goods involved, are systematically extended."[4] Preaching, I believe, is such a practice since it is essential to the church's very being. The church preaches because by its very nature the church cannot do otherwise. Preaching is not an activity done for some other purpose, some other reason, that is not already intrinsic to preaching itself. Accordingly, preaching requires and develops virtue in a community sufficient to sustaining preaching as essential for what that community is about, which is but a reminder that preaching is

---

3. Stanley M. Hauerwas, *After Christendom?* (Nashville: Abingdon, 1991), 93–112. I develop the ecclesial significance of this point in my *In Good Company: The Church as Polis* (forthcoming from University of Notre Dame Press).

4. Alasdair C. MacIntyre, *After Virtue*, 2d ed. (Notre Dame, Ind.: University of Notre Dame Press, 1984), 187.

fundamentally a political activity insofar as the church, through its preaching ministry, discovers the good we have in common.

It may still be objected that the idea that we ought to try to practice preaching does not seem like a good one. Most congregations would not want to be subject to someone "practicing preaching." Most crafts require that beginners learn to practice, but few of us desire to be the guinea pigs on whom such beginners practice. Surgeons must be initiated into the craft of surgery by operating on someone for the first time, but few of us wish to be that patient.

Yet, the analogy of surgery is wrong for preaching. For as I suggested above using MacIntyre's account of practice, we must remember that preaching is not what a preacher does, but rather it is the activity of the whole community. Preaching as practice is the activity of the church that requires the church to be as able listeners, as well-schooled and well-crafted hearers, as the preacher is the proclaimer. Indeed, I suspect one of the great difficulties of preaching in the church today is the preachers' presumption that those to whom they preach do not have ears well trained to hear. As a result, preaching is not the practice of the community but rather, as it so often is, an exercise in sentimentality.

The Authority of the Practice

Preaching as the practice of the whole church is an authoritative practice. Through the proclamation of the gospel, the church stands joyfully under the authority of the Word. Preaching as a practice of the whole community, therefore, can never be understood as that time when preachers give their opinions about this or that or share with a congregation unique or peculiar insights they have learned. You know, or the one to whom you are listening knows, that you have abandoned preaching authoritatively if the sermon involves telling the church some bit of the wisdom discovered through our children. That is the surest sign the sermon is not the practice of the church and has become instead an exercise meant to reinforce middle-class religiosity.

For preaching to be a practice intrinsic to the worship of God requires that the preacher, as well as the congregation, stand under the authority of the Word. That is why preaching should rightly follow a lectionary. To preach from the lectionary makes clear that preaching is the work of the church and not some arbitrary decision by the minister to find a text to fit a peculiar theme that currently fits the preacher's subjectivity. Rather, the exercise of the ministry of proclamation requires ministers to make clear that the Word preached is as painful to them as it is to the congregation. Such an acknowledgment makes clear that preaching is not just another speech but rather the way this people, including the preacher, is formed into the Word of God.

The practice of preaching as the practice of authority, particularly in our culture, cannot help but be prophetic. It is a mistake to think that prophetic preaching occurs when the preacher holds up a specific moral challenge to the congregation. On the contrary, preaching as a practice is prophetic when it is done with authority. Where else in our culture do you find a people gathered in obedience to a Word they know they will not easily hear?

Such an exercise of authority is anomalous in liberal cultures, which assume that all forms of authority cannot help but be authoritarian. As I have put the matter elsewhere, the story of modernity is that we should have no story except the story we chose when we had no story.[5] People schooled in that story cannot help but think no one has the right to stand in authority over them. So the very idea that they should be trained to be faithful hearers of the Word proclaimed seems anomalous.

It is important to note that this is not simply another attack on American individualism. To be sure, we live in a destructively individualistic culture and society. But I have put the issue in the language of story exactly because I think it illumines our difficulties better than the notion of individualism. The difficulty is not that we are just individualistic but that we believe that there is actually a place from which we can choose our story. That, of course, is a story that we did not choose and that determines us to be people who are interminably self-deceived.

In contrast, preaching as the practice of the church is a constant reminder that the church is constituted by people who have learned that they have not chosen God. Rather, we are a people who have been chosen by God, which, at the very least, means we discover that

---

5. Stanley M. Hauerwas, *Dispatches from the Front: Theological Engagements with the Secular* (Durham, N.C.: Duke University Press, 1994), 164–76.

we are a people constituted by a story that we have not chosen. This is a story we could not have "made up." Accordingly, to be a good hearer, to practice preaching, requires that we be schooled to be creatures. To be a creature means we must learn that our lives are gifts of a gracious God. I do not say that we receive our lives as a gift because that would mean we already existed prior to the reception of our lives as a gift. The fact is that our very lives are a gift. That we are so constituted requires the constant practice that comes through receiving the Word of God through preaching.

So preaching as one of the essential practices of Christian worship is a prophetic reminder to a culture bent on denying our status as creature. In preaching, the church has been given the gift of prophecy and is made more than it could otherwise be. As in the account of practice suggested above by MacIntyre, we know we are made more than we could ever imagine through preaching. That is why, I suspect, those who are set aside for the preaching ministry of the church often discover they acquire a power they did not know they had by being forced to proclaim the Word of God. To acknowledge that power can be frightening as we fear what it may mean for our lives. The joy, however, is to know what it will mean for the upbuilding of the whole church as God makes us more than we could ever be through the proclamation of God's Word.

The Story That Requires That Preaching Be Practiced

It should be obvious that preaching as a practice required by and for the church is not separable from what preaching is about. Preaching is the proclamation of the Word of God as found in the people of Israel and the life, death, and resurrection of Jesus of Nazareth. Preaching, therefore, is the practice that is meant to help us locate our lives in God's story. To do that, preaching must be about God's story through the explication of the Scripture. Scripture is, of course, composed of many stories — all of which, the church has taught us, help illumine the gospel.[6]

---

6. As Robert Jenson puts it, "The story of the sermon and the hymns and of the processions and of the sacramental acts and of the readings is to be God's story, the story of the Bible. Preachers are the greatest sinners here: the text already is and belongs to the one true story; it does not need to be helped out in this respect. What is said and enacted in the church must be

In the introduction to William Willimon's and my book *Preaching to Strangers*, I suggested that most preaching today fits what George Limbeck has characterized as an experimental-expressivist view of religion.[7] The fundamental assumption of the experimental-expressivist view is that different religions are diverse expressions of a common experience. Such a view, of course, has been the very center of Protestant liberal theology as exemplified by such theologians as Paul Tillich and Reinhold Niebuhr. From this perspective, the gospel is seen as a provocative account of the human condition. Such theology, and the preaching that it produces, can be extraordinarily powerful as well as popular in a culture formed by the story that one should have no story except the story one chooses when one has no story.

Moreover, preaching in the experimental-expressivist mode can be quite artful. Literary examples are a natural resource as the preacher oftentimes finds Kahil Gibran more insightful than the Gospel of Mark. Moreover, such a view of preaching seems better able to show the relevance of preaching to the "real-life situations" of people as well as to contemporary social problems.

But for all its aesthetic and artful qualities, such preaching is not the practice of preaching required by the church. That practice is proclamation since it requires that the preacher and hearers be confronted by a Word that does not illumine what they already know but rather tells us what we do not know — and, indeed, could not know on our own. That is why it must be done over and over again. Repetition is the key to helping us understand the material content of what it is we practice when we preach. It is the practice of the story of God that is not about the illumination of the human condition but rather about the proclamation of God found in the people of Israel and the life of Jesus of Nazareth. These are not general truths but rather a story that can be known only through hearing it proclaimed amidst that body of people gathered in the hopes that we will be faithful hearers of God's story.

Preaching is that practice meant to help us locate our lives, our sto-

---

with the greatest exactitude and faithfulness and exclusivity the story of creation and redemption by the God of Israel and Father of the Risen Christ." See Jenson, "How the World Lost Its Story," *First Things* 36 (October 1993): 22.

7. William H. Willimon and Stanley M. Hauerwas, *Preaching to Strangers* (Louisville: Westminster/John Knox, 1992), 1–13.

ries, in God's story. But preaching is not meant to stand alone; rather, it is surrounded by and sustained within the whole liturgy of the church. Preaching is that part of the church's liturgy through which we are reminded of the story that shapes all that we do from gathering to sending forth. That is why preaching finally requires it be sealed by that other practice essential to worship, that is, the Eucharist. Word and table are forever bound together as those practices necessary for us to understand we are the baptized people of God. Through baptism we have been made the people of God capable of that strange but wonderful practice called preaching. What a wonderful gift.

5

EMBODIED MEMORY
Acts 5:27-32; Rev. 1:4-8; John 20:19-31

Stanley M. Hauerwas

It is currently fashionable to be a victim. In order to have status to-day, it seems we must have in our life some peculiar misfortune that we can claim should give us special consideration. It is also currently fashionable to reject claims of victimization. That at least seems to be the case in any reading of our current politics. White middle-class males (people like me), it seems, have had it with the whiners. We've worked hard, done well enough, and we will be damned if we want to apologize for it. We do not mean to be unfeeling. In fact, we are sorry that certain people have suffered past wrongs, but we did not perpetrate those wrongs, and we see no reason that we should be held accountable.

For example, here in the South, we know that slavery certainly existed, and racism was a terrible reality that is still, unfortunately, too much with us. Look around — we are not an all-white church by accident. Yet we did not own slaves; certainly my people did not own slaves. We were poor whites, and we suffered as much as African Americans. Moreover, while racism is still certainly present, we do not think ourselves to be racist, so we refuse to believe we have anything for which we should apologize and/or anything we should change in our own lives.

Current claims about victimization make it difficult to remember the Holocaust, as we are asked to do on the Sunday after Easter, for to remember the destruction of the Jews can too easily be seen as just another victim's strategy to make us feel guilty. Moreover, it seems an odd day to be asked to remember the Holocaust since it seems nothing distances us more from the Jews than the resurrection — a view I hope to counter by the end of this sermon by reminding us that nothing is more Jewish than Jesus' bodily resurrection.

However, at least one of the reasons we have to remember the Holocaust is that fifty years ago, on April 9 to be exact, the great theologian Dietrich Bonhoeffer was hanged by the Nazis for his resistance to Hitler. We rightly celebrate Bonhoeffer's life, but such a celebration can tempt us to avoid the issue of Christian complicity with the Holocaust. That some Christians resisted the destruction of European Jewry does not mean that we can forget the centuries of Christian persecution of the Jews that led to the horrible destruction at Auschwitz and Belsen.

But, just as many of us react against some of the current rhetoric of victimization, we also react against attempts to make us remember the Holocaust. After all, we American Christians did not perpetrate the Holocaust. We were and are a tolerant society. We fought to end the Holocaust. Is not the Holocaust like slavery? — that is, a terrible thing, but not really part of our lives. Why should we be asked to remember such events? Those that would force such remembering assume wrongly that such remembrance will prevent the recurrence of anti-Semitism or racism.

Still we Christians must remember the Holocaust. We have no choice. We must also remember slavery, though remembering slavery is different from remembering the Holocaust. Yet I hope to suggest that if we get straight what it means to remember the Holocaust, we will better know how to remember slavery.

What is crucial about our remembering the Holocaust is, of course, the special relationship to Judaism that we have as Christians. For our Christ, the Jesus we worship, was and is the Savior of Israel. For example, notice in the text from Acts for today, when Peter and some of the other followers of Jesus were brought before the high priest of the temple in Jerusalem, the high priest notes they had prohibited Peter and the apostles from teaching in Jesus' name, assuming that in so teaching they were trying to blame the priests for Jesus' death — they are the enemies of victimization in their day. Peter responds, as the prophets had responded, that when God requires that God's apostles speak, they can do nothing other than speak. Moreover, it is the God of those same prophets who has raised the crucified Jesus. That same

God, Peter claims, "exalted him at his right hand as Leader and Savior, to give repentance to Israel and forgiveness of sins" (Acts 5:31 RSV). Note that it is to Israel that Jesus has given repentance and forgiveness of sins. It was not to us — that is, we Gentiles — that the promise first came; forgiveness is first offered to Israel.

Here in Acts we see reflected Paul's claim in Romans 11 that God has by no means rejected his people, Israel. God's promises are good and true, and our salvation continues to depend upon Israel and the Jews as God's promised people. As Paul says, "Through their trespass salvation has come to the Gentiles, so as to make Israel jealous. Now if their trespass means riches for the world, and if their failure means riches for the Gentiles, how much more will their full inclusion mean!" (Rom. 11:11–12 RSV).

Of course, as Christian history has developed, Christian envy of the Jew for being God's promised people has reaped horrible results. Christians, a resurrection people, are never quite sure of what to make of the fact that the Jews remain God's people. Our calling, which was meant to make the Jews jealous, turned out to make Christians envious and hateful. Ironically, this has resulted in Jews living more faithfully to the way of Jesus than Christians themselves. For what people other than the Jews have remained steadfast to loyalty to God? It is the Jews who have learned to survive across the centuries in faithful remembrance and worship of God — without an army. They, after all, have lived more like Christians than Christians ever could — which is but a reminder that when all is said and done, all this is about God and what God has made possible.

The Jews have not needed an army because they have had something better — memory. They have had a memory, moreover, that is, not some flimsy set of mental images, but a memory embodied in the unavoidable flesh of a people, a memory determined by law, by land, by worship. Thus even a nonpracticing Jew remains a Jew, as God simply will not let them go. God's refusal to let the Jew go is the way God has chosen to grace lives with the memory that we are God's good creatures.

That the Jews have lived as a people by memory is a reminder that we Christians also live by memory. We do not just live by memory, but, in fact, we are memory, as we become part of God's very life through eucharistic sacrifice so that the world may know our God is the God who called Abraham from Ur of the Chaldeans and has remained faithful to the promises to Israel. In fact, that is what our worship is — that is, it is a participation in God's remembering that the world may know that God has not and will not abandon God's good creation.

This is the reason we Christians cannot forget the horror of the Holocaust. We cannot forget it because it is not just history; it is not just something that happened to the Jews in Europe in the recent past. Rather, we cannot forget the Holocaust because it must now be part of the Christian story, the Christian memory, just as Israel is always part of our story.

In the second century of the common era, Marcion, a Christian Gnostic, suggested that the Old Testament should be left behind and only snatches of the Gospel of Luke and the Pauline Epistles should be our Scripture. In brief, Marcion wanted to free the church of the Jews and, in particular, the God of the Jews. The God of the Jews, the God of what we now call the *Old Testament*, Marcion thought far too material, too concerned with law and vengeance. Marcion thought resurrection meant that Jesus had freed us of the need for body and of the necessity of memory carried by our baptized bodies. The church decisively rejected Marcion's attempt to create a pure Christianity free of the people of Israel because the church saw clearly that Jesus is no mere idea, but the resurrected Jesus is the fleshly embodiment of Israel. To forget Israel would be nothing less than to lose the body and blood of our Savior's life made present to us through resurrection and ascension. To forget Israel would mean that our Eucharist would be nothing but another meal.

Christianity is no universal truth that can be known in and out of itself. Rather, what it means to be Christian is to know that God is known through the Jews and through this Jesus. That memory involves much terror. Ask the Canaanites, for example. Many today celebrate Israel's exodus from Egypt and the conquest of Canaan as "liberation," but the Canaanites did not feel liberated. Our history is filled with violence that we suppress in order to comfort ourselves that our God has really gotten over all that "unpleasantness." But such unpleasantness cannot be left behind. In the name of our gentle Savior, we Christians have perpetrated horrible crimes — holocausts — that must be remembered.

But how do you remember something as terrible as the Holocaust? What was perpetrated there was surely so wrong that nothing can ever make it right. We can see a movie like *Schindler's List* and celebrate the triumph of the human spirit, in particular a spirit such as Schindler's, over such terror, but such a triumph is small comfort against six million deaths. The deep difficulty, in other words, is how to remember the horror of the Holocaust or of slavery without telling yourself lies about such terror — (e.g., things really worked out all right in the long run). No, things have not worked out well in the long run. That they did not is why we are stuck in unending debate about who has been the most wronged.

Which brings us to our Gospel text for today. This text is often used to reassure ourselves that the resurrection really happened. We come to this text as people who are a bit embarrassed that we believe in Jesus' resurrection because it just seems so, well, unusual — particularly for modern people like us. When candid, we identify with Thomas — we want proof of this thing called *resurrection*. As modern people we confuse resurrection with resuscitation of a corpse, and we think that this text is an attempt to reassure us that such a resuscitation really happened. We think, like Thomas, that if we could just see those wounded hands and that side with its spear gash, we would really be assured that this thing really happened.

Resurrection is not, however, about the resuscitation of a corpse. What was extraordinary about the resurrection is not that a dead man returned from the dead but that this man Jesus is the Lord's anointed who has, through resurrection, the power to forgive sins. Note that when Jesus appears to the apostles, his great work is that he breathes on them and says, "Receive the Holy Spirit. If you forgive the sins of any, they are forgiven; if you retain the sins of any, they are retained" (John 20:22-23 RSV). Only God has the power to forgive sins, but here we see that our Jesus has that power. That is the reason we know resurrection is, not the resuscitation of a dead corpse, but rather the sign that says Jesus is the second person of the Trinity who has the power to forgive sins — a power that has now been frighteningly given to us.

Thomas on being confronted with Jesus, on seeing that this resurrected one is the crucified one, makes the extraordinary response, "My Lord and my God!" What a strange response. You would think, given our assumption about "proof," he might have said something like, "Oh! You've come back." But that is not what he said. Rather, what he said is that this is the one with the power to forgive sins. It turns out it was not "proof" Thomas was after but lordship. Resurrection is about God's triumph over life determined by unending vengeance. God has the power to forgive sins, which of course is absolutely essential if we are to be a people of memory.

The great trick of being Christian, the magic of what it means to be who we are, is that we know ourselves to be a forgiven and reconciled people. We know as a people of memory that we must remember horrors so terrible we wish to repress and deny that they ever existed exactly because they cannot be made right. When you are part of a history, a memory as horrible as the Holocaust, as slavery, there is nothing that can be done to make it right. The great temptation is to let time wash it away, to let it become a matter of forgetfulness — thus, we say, "Time heals all wounds." Accordingly, we Americans try to deal with slavery and the genocide against Native Americans by relegating that all to the past. African Americans and native peoples, we say, should quit using those terrors to produce guilt. After all, now we have civil rights, so what's a little slavery between friends? We have tried to make up for part of the wrongs with affirmative-action policies, though we, that is, we white people, have to confess that we are beginning to tire a bit of trying to be fair.

Yet we Christians remember, not because we like to wallow in guilt, but because we know we have been forgiven and thus have been made truthful rememberers. Such remembering, moreover, saves us from being the eternal victim. For we know as Christians that we have been freed from being victimized because our Savior has defeated death and death's lies. We have been made part of God's great communion of saints, so those who would kill us can never determine who we are. Moreover, we know affirmative action can never be a substitute for penance, forgiveness, and reconciliation. For what penance and reconciliation name is the process through which we learn that the story of those we have harmed or who have harmed us cannot be forgotten since our God is the God of the Jews — they could never forget the Canaanites.

Therefore we remember that once we were no people, but now, through resurrection, we are God's people — indeed, as we are told from Revelation, through his blood we have been made a kingdom of priests, which is to say that we are a people who have been made what we are by faithful memory. No doubt, at Jesus' trial we would have been among those crying, "Crucify him! Crucify him!" — but through the power of the Holy Spirit God has made us part of God's people so that the world may know that we need not forget the terror of Christ's crucifixion. For in forgetting the terror, we too often are prone to repeat it through attempts to make it right in order to assure our righteousness. Such strategies are left behind by our being a people who have received the Holy Spirit and thus are capable of being a forgiven people and, accordingly, are capable of forgiveness. Only such a people can truthfully remember our sins; only such a people can live through memory, a memory that is no longer self-justifying but righteous. How wonderful it is to be a part of such a people.

What a story we have to tell the world. What a different politics we have to hold up to the world — a politics of memory not governed by blame and guilt. Surely a people capable of being a forgiving people, capable of remembering the Holocaust, will be blessed to God — yet do not expect the world to praise us for such remembering. The world does not want to be reminded. But what could be better news than to be God's people — that is, a people called to witness to God's triumph over the terror of the world's forgetfulness by being made participants in God's memory?

6

HATING MOTHERS AS THE WAY TO PEACE

Ezek. 33:1–11; Philemon 1:1–20; Luke 14:25–33

STANLEY M. HAUERWAS

I've been asked to write on preaching on the "peaceable kingdom." Rather than write about preaching on the topic, I would prefer to provide an example of how I tried to preach the peaceable kingdom. I was asked to preach at the United Methodist Church in Pittsboro, North Carolina, the Sunday they were to read the Methodist bishops' pastoral on nuclear war. I simply used the lectionary text appointed for that Sunday, and the following sermon resulted. I hope it manifests my conviction that "peace" is, not a subject abstracted from the gospel, but rather is intrinsic to what we believe the salvation wrought in and by Jesus is about.

Most of us believe we are nonviolent. We believe that we would prefer to be peaceable rather than violent in most circumstances of our lives. Violence is something we believe exists "out there" in criminal behavior or in relations between states. We simply do not believe it is in our souls. Rather, violence is in structures of our existence insofar as they are determined by past and ongoing justice.

Moreover, there is some basis for this belief. Few of us have ever threatened anyone with physical violence. We may entertain heroic fantasies of responding to or employing violence in a good cause. But most of us discover that if we are actually confronted with violence and need to respond in kind, we become physically ill. We simply are not natural killers. We sincerely prefer to live in order rather than in the disorder that violence always seems to breed.

It is very hard indeed to get us to kill. This is true even in war, as it was discovered in World War I that 40 percent of the soldiers in combat never fired their weapons. That is the reason the military created the platoon system, as there are friendships created that force us finally to use violence in the protection of one another. As Jay Glenn Gray notes in his wonderful book *The Warriors*, "Numberless soldiers have died more or less willingly, not for country or religious faith or for any other abstract good, but because they realized that by fleeing their post and rescuing themselves they would expose their companions to greater danger. Such loyalty is the essence of fighting morale."[1] So even in war we discover that we are not violent in ourselves, but only because we so care about those we learned to love by being exposed to a common danger.

In short, we kill to protect others. In that sense our psychology seems to fit Augustine's defense of the use of violence through war. Augustine argued it is incompatible for a Christian to use violence for personal protection. Thus, his defense of the just war was never on grounds that it was analogous to self-defense. Rather, Augustine argued that Christians can only use violence to protect the innocent, and by innocent he only meant those who did not deserve the attack they were receiving. So the Christian justification of violence does not derive from the assumption that we at times cannot avoid defending ourselves; rather, violence is necessary if we are charitably to protect the innocent.

All of which reminds us that our violence lies not in ourselves but in our loves. We think it crucial to protect those we love. Indeed, I suspect most of us go to war to protect our loves. Our families, our neighborhoods, are what we care about when we go to war — nations are but symbols of those cares. Moreover, there seems to be something deeply right about this. It is natural to defend those we love, and we have little use for those who did not feel they should so defend those they love. Cowardice, in fact, is to place our interest in survival over those we love. It is only on this basis that we can understand why war is such an important moral institution, as without it we would lack the means of sacrifice so crucial for us to know how important our loves are to us.

I suspect this is the reason the gospel text above is so jarring: "If

---

1. Jay Glenn Gray, *The Warriors* (New York: Harcourt Brace, 1959).

anyone comes to me and does not hate his own father and mother and wife and children and brothers and sisters, yes, and even his own life, he cannot be my disciple" (Luke 14:25 RSV). On hearing this hard word, we think that Jesus must surely be speaking figuratively — after all, if Christianity is about anything today, we think it must surely be about supporting the family. What Jesus must mean, therefore, is that we must not love our families too much. He is simply recommending that we need to get our priorities right. We should remember to not make our families God. But once we remember that, it is surely right to love our families even to the taking of the life of others, if necessary, to defend them.

Yet that is not what the text says. It does not say that we've merely got our priorities wrong. Rather, it says that now that we are in the presence of Jesus Christ, all our relations have been transvalued. In the death and resurrection of this man, a great reversal has taken place, causing all our natural loves to be transformed.

This is the beginning of a new age — an age that we do not become part of unless we hate mother, hate father, hate wife and children. This is not just a matter of getting our priorities straight. No, it means that now everything has been returned to its original purpose. The new age is here in the person of Jesus Christ. We are no longer under the powers of the old age — powers that feed on our fears and our loves so that we are led to kill other people's children in the name of protecting our children. Hate mother, hate father, hate wife and children, only makes sense if we now live in a new time where everything is made new. The wolf will now lie down with the lamb, and we can love our children without threatening the children of others.

Indeed, Jesus argues in a quite commonsense way that when you are going to build a tower, you would be pretty silly to begin without knowing if you had the resources to complete it. So, should you only get the foundation done, you will be mocked, for your neighbors will say, "What a silly person to have begun a project without knowing whether the resources were available to complete it." Raised the son of a bricklayer, I think I can understand just how silly we would be to start such a project.

Or again, Jesus suggests that those who encounter another in war had better make sure they have the soldiers to win. To enter war, the most serious of business, facing certain defeat would surely be silly.

If you confront unfavorable odds, you certainly ought to sue for peace before you begin the battle. Otherwise, many people will sacrifice their lives for no good reason.

The purpose of these examples is not to give recommendations about how to be a better builder and/or general. The point is that if Jesus is the Messiah, it is surely absurd to think we can follow Jesus while clinging to the attachments of the old age. Rather, to be his disciple means that all our past, all our loves — the loves of our mothers, our fathers, our wives and children — are now put in a new context. We have become part of a new kingdom that makes it possible for our loves to be the basis of peace rather than the source of our violence. For in this new age we love, knowing our security is in God, who has redeemed time through the establishment of his kingdom in Jesus. We no longer need desperately try to ensure the survival of those we love, for we can now love them with the security and the conviction that God's kingdom is surely here. In short, Jesus brought the end time so that we may have the time to love without that love becoming the source of our violence.

Putting this as dramatically as I can leads me to equate Jesus' claim about the end time with a nuclear war. Imagine yourself surviving a nuclear war. Imagine yourself being one of the survivors of Hiroshima or Nagasaki. We can hardly imagine what that would feel like, but we know that surely everything — even our loves — would be forever changed. Common testimony of those at Hiroshima is that after the bomb they were numb, feeling nothing. Moreover, even as their feelings returned, their lives were forever scarred by that event. Everything they did afterward was in reference to their being survivors. The bomb had scarred their history, transfiguring past and future. Each individual had to learn to love as a survivor. In short, they had to learn to cherish one another under the dreadful knowledge of what happened then and what perhaps awaited in the future.

But as Christians we believe that what happened in Jesus Christ was more dramatic than what happened at Hiroshima or even what would happen if there were a nuclear exchange between America and some other nation. For what happened in Jesus Christ is that God sent his Son to reclaim his creation, and we killed him. It is often said today that there is nothing we could do that is worse than destroying the human species through a nuclear war. That is surely wrong. We have already done the worst thing we could do. We killed him who would work our redemption. That is the worst thing that humankind could possibly do.

But the good news is that the God we crucified refused to let our "no" be the final word. God refused to hold this horrible sin against us. Raising Jesus from the grave, God rejects our rejection. Instead, God offers us the opportunity to become part of a new kingdom — of a new time — so that the world might know its true sovereign. It is a time that creates the space for us to learn to love one another, so now our loves will not become the excuse to kill in the name of those loves. For now we have learned that the very heart of love is a nonviolence, as God has come not to coerce us into loving. Rather, because God has made it possible for us to freely respond to this love, we become new creatures.

It is no wonder, therefore, that we believe as Christians what has happened in Jesus Christ is more significant than even a nuclear war — that we believe what has happened in Jesus Christ has changed all our relations. But this "bomb" that is our redemption does not leave us numb as the bomb at Hiroshima left the survivors there. On the contrary, this bomb empowers us to witness to the world what good news it is that God has rejected our rejection. God uses our sin to offer us a new life, free from the fear that fuels our violence. For now we know that God has removed the violence that once lay in our loves, as we have been taught to love one another, not in general but in Christ. Only that love can be the love of peace, for we can love not fearing its loss. Rather, we can be confident that now our loves rightly build Christ's kingdom, which is the only alternative to the world's kingdom of war.

This is the gospel. This is what makes it possible for us to be at peace — to be a peaceable people — in a world at war. For we Christians know we must be peaceable people — in a world at war. We don't believe that we should be peaceable because our peace is a political strategy for freeing the world from war; rather, we Christians know we must be peaceable because our peace is the only way that we can live in a world at war.

This kind of living, of course, is what we do here as we worship God. Through our worship we proclaim to the world we are a people in service to God, so we take the time — even in a world at war — to share in God's peace, wishing one another a share in that same peace. We know the world in its feverish attempt to make peace a reality would have us kill in the name of such peace. Yet we know there cannot be a peace we share with one another before coming to share God's life in the Eucharist.

That is what we do here as we celebrate God's peace. Here we become brothers and sisters caring for one another in Christ. We care for one another not in family bloodlines but in Christ. The blood of the cross has forever qualified the blood of the family, making it impossible for us to spill the blood of others in the name of our families. This new eschatological family we call the church now has our fundamental loyalty that makes possible the peace, even among families.

For example, much today is said about domestic violence. The causes of this horrible phenomenon are no doubt many and complex. But surely one of the reasons we seem so incapable of providing an alternative for such violence is that we have no way of providing, apart from the family, a paradigm of love that is genuinely peaceable. If we are to love one another well in the family — as husband and wives, as brothers and sisters, as parents and children — we need a sense of a love that is at once nonviolent and truthful. Such love cannot be real without our family's loves being fundamentally qualified by the love that we learned in the church.

I am aware that this is an extraordinary and perhaps even frightening thing to say, but then God is a frightening presence. Indeed, from this perspective I suspect some of us begin to have just a little sympathy for those who put Jesus to death. How dare Jesus tell me to hate my father, my mother, and especially my children! Yet that is exactly what he said we must do if we are to be part of God's kingdom of peace and love. For any love that does not love the other relative to the God who has loved us is now accursed. Any love that does not love in the manner that God loves us in Jesus of Nazareth will only be as such a cause of our violence, as it provides the needed rationale to unleash the vengeance of the wrongs others do to those we love.

This is indeed a hard saying, but the message is still harder. As we learn from the passage in Ezekiel, God's watchman can be tempted not to sound the warning. Moreover, if we fail to warn, then the very iniquity of those we are called to warn is ours. These are frightening words indeed for those of us who would bear the name *Christian*. For we believe Christ has made us, his church, the watchman for the world. Our task is to sound the horn that the world might be warned that its ways lead only to its own destruction.

Yet the extent of violence in the world, the *mad* situation in which we find ourselves in regard to nuclear weapons, is but a sign of the church's failure to be God's watchman — to be God's horn blower. The church's task is not to warn the world that it stands on the brink of destroying itself through nuclear war. The world knows that. You can read about that in the *New York Times*. Rather, the church's task is to tell the world that the reason it is so violent is because of its unbelief and that its loves are thereby perverted. For the world does not believe that Jesus has in fact risen, making present a new age and thus transforming our lives. The world does not believe in a God who refuses to let our rejection of Jesus determine our relations to God and to one another. We must say to the world, as watchmen, that we see the sword and that all that is the world must turn from unbelief. We must learn to love our lives as gifts and not as possessions. We must learn to love those who are so important to us as gifts from God and not as our possessions. Only then will the world have an alternative to the world's violence.

It is good news indeed, as we hear in Ezekiel, that God takes no pleasure in our death but, instead, calls us to life as his church in order that the world might know there is an alternative to our violence. Church statements against nuclear war will do little to make the bomb go away. But that is not the church's task. Our task is to watch and blow the warnings, that we and the world might know God has redeemed us in Jesus Christ in a manner that nothing we do — even the destruction of the world — can remove. Let us praise God for that — even for being led time and time again to God's table of sacrifice where our loves are transformed, so that rather than being the source of violence, our loves become the exemplification of God's peace. Amen.

. . . That is how I preached on the peaceable kingdom.

7

PREACHING THE TERRORS

Barbara Brown Taylor

Not long ago, I was invited to address a senior citizens' group on "Women in the Old Testament." They had been studying various biblical characters and wanted me to introduce them to some of Israel's heroines, so I did. I told them about Jael, "most blessed of women" (Judg. 5:24), who drove a tent peg through Sisera's temple with a mallet. I told them about Judith, who seduced Holofernes and then paused to pray—"Give me strength today, O Lord God of Israel!"—before plunging his own sword into his neck (Judith 13:7). I told them about Esther, who won permission for the Jews of her husband's Persian empire "to destroy, to kill, and to annihilate" seventy-five thousand of their enemies (Esther 8:11). By the end of my talk, my audience's eyes were very large, and I was feeling a little queasy myself. They thanked me very much and have never asked me back.

Now granted, I could just as easily have talked about Sarah, Ruth, and the widow of Zarephath, but there comes a time in every preacher's life when the queasy-making parts of the Bible can no longer be ignored, when it is time to admit that the Bible is not a book about admirable people or even about a conventionally admirable God. It is instead a book about a sovereign God's covenant with a chosen people, as full of holy terrors as it is of holy wonders, none of which we may avoid without avoiding part of the truth.

On the whole, we do not do so well with the terror part. It does not fit the image of God we wish to publish; it goes against the good news we want to proclaim. In these days of dwindling numbers, who is eager to remind the congregation how the prophet Elisha cursed a crowd of jeering boys in the name of the Lord and how two she-bears trundled obediently out of the woods to maul forty-two of them (2 Kings 2:23–25)? Or how Ananias and Sapphira were struck dead for withholding a portion of their cash from the early Christian community (Acts 5:1–11)?

Fortunately, or unfortunately, there is little reason to tangle with such peripheral texts of terror when we have much more central texts readily at hand. In the Old Testament, God asks Abraham to roast his only son; in the New Testament, God's will puts another only son on a cross. In these two worst-case scenarios and all their derivatives, the issue for us remains the same: how do we preach a loving God who does such unloving things? How do we preach the terrors?

In practice, we tend to preach them by making them less terrible. Of course God sent a ram to take Isaac's place at the last moment, we say; of course God raised Jesus from the dead and made him Lord of all. Thus the first story becomes one about how obedience results in rescue, and the second one, a story about how obedience results in resurrection, but what is lost while such morals are being made is the very real terror of obeying God without the least idea how things will turn out in the end — which is, after all, the human situation. Things will turn out according to God's will, certainly, and in faith we confess that to be enough for us. But insofar as God's will is so radically different from our own, there is plenty of room for terror in our lives.

Every preacher has his or her own canon of terror. My own includes three kinds of texts: first, those in which God sanctions violence — killing every firstborn in the land of Egypt (Exod. 11:5) or ordering Saul to slaughter the Amalekites down to the last woman, child, and donkey (1 Sam. 15:3); second, those in which God aims to separate me from my stuff — suggesting that I surrender my last handful of meal (1 Kings 17:12) or sell all that I own (Mark 10:21); and third, those texts in which God exercises final judgment — refusing to open the door to the foolish bridesmaids (Matt. 25:12) or banishing the ill-clad wedding guest to outer darkness where there is weeping and gnashing of teeth (Matt. 22:13). These are terrible to me because they expose my vulnerability. If God can condemn Amalekite babies for the sins of their parents, then there is no hope for me. Nor can I find safety in following Jesus if selling all that I own is the way. So of course I will find myself on the wrong side of the door when the times comes, hearing my muffled sentence pronounced through the latch: "Truly, I tell you, I do not know you." These are terrible texts because they remind me how helpless I am, how frail and not in charge I am. While there are clearly things I can do to improve my life and things I can do to cheapen it, my fate is ultimately out of my hands. I cannot control God's disposition toward me, and that is terrifying.

One way to hide from such knowledge is to take refuge in righteousness, suggesting that those who behave properly are terror-exempt. Obey God and avoid the sword. Give generously and avoid misfortune. Be good sheep and dodge the outer darkness. Congregations are relieved to hear sermons like these, and preachers are glad to preach them because they offer some leverage in an otherwise frightening universe, but they finally fail to meet the test either of human experience or biblical witness. Job stands on one side of the pulpit shaking his head, and Jesus on the other, both of them confirming our fear that righteousness does nothing to dissuade God from trying the faithful by fire and by ice.

That, finally, is what makes a text terrible to me — not what it exposes about me but what it exposes about God — a sovereign God who is radically different from me, whose mind I cannot read, whose decisions I cannot predict, whose actions I cannot control. "It is a fearful thing to fall into the hands of the living God," writes the author of the Letter to the Hebrews (10:31), but it is not as if we had a choice. That is whose hands we are in; our only choice is how we will handle our fear.

As preachers we have an additional choice, and that is how we will address the fear of those who listen to us. Jonathan Edwards, the great eighteenth-century American revivalist, was one of the most frightening preachers of all time. In his book *Thoughts on the Revival of Religion in New England*, he rose to the defense of those who were being blamed for "speaking terror to them that are already under great terrors."[1] It was, he said, a matter of saving those who were drowning in full sight of land.

A person that sees himself ready to sink into hell is ready to strive, some way or other, to lay God under some obligation to him; but he is to be beat off from everything of that nature,

---

1. Richard Lischer, ed., *Theories of Preaching* (Durham, N.C.: Labyrinth, 1987), 100.

though it greatly increases his terror to see himself wholly des-
titute, on every side, of any refuge, or any thing of his own to
lay hold of; as a man that sees himself in danger of drowning is
in terror and endeavors to catch hold on every twig within his
reach, and he that pulls away those twigs from him increases his
terror; yet if they are insufficient to save him, and by being in
his way prevent his looking to that which will save him, to pull
them away is necessary to save his life.[2]

It is an alarming image, and yet it is what texts of terror do. They
pry our fingers away from our own ideas about who God should be
and how God should act so that there are only two things left for us
to do with our fear: use it to propel us toward the God who is, or let
it sink us like a stone. Preaching texts of terror calls for the same kind
of choice. We may try to protect ourselves and our congregations from
them by tossing out inflatable bits of comfort and advice, or we may
find the courage to forsake those twigs and swim for our lives toward
the living God. As fearful as that may be, it is finally less fearful than
the alternative.

In a paradoxical way, texts of terror carry their own consolation
inside of them. Several nights ago a friend and I watched Laurence
Olivier in Shakespeare's *King Lear*. Neither of us had ever seen the
play before, so we were unprepared for the relentless tragedy of it,
with fathers rejecting children, children betraying parents, brothers
plotting against brothers, and sisters poisoning sisters. By the end of
the last scene, the stage was littered with bodies — Lear, Cordelia,
Goneril, Regan, Edmund — all dead. As the lights went down and
the credits rolled, my friend turned to me with tears in his eyes and
said, "What could be more wonderful than that?"

When I asked him to explain himself, he could not, except to say
that he recognized his own life in the play and that it helped him
somehow to see his worst fears acted out. It was real — that was the
best he could do — and it was redemptive for him to witness real pain
suffered in a way that seemed true to him. In the same way, I believe,
texts of terror are recognizable to us. Judgment, violence, rejection,
death — they are all present in our world if not in our lives, and there
is some crazy kind of consolation in the fact that they are present

---

2. Ibid., 102.

in the Bible as well. They remind us that the Bible is not all lambs and rainbows. If it were, it would not be our book. Our book has everything in it — wonder and terrors, worst fears and best hopes — both for ourselves and our relationship with God. The best hope of all is that because the terrors are included here, as part of the covenant story, they may turn out to be redemptive in the end, when we see dimly no more but face to face at last.

That is the fundamental hope all texts of terror drive us to: that however wrong they may seem to us, however misbegotten and needlessly cruel, God may yet be present in them, working redemption in ways we are not equipped to discern. Our fear of God's method may turn out to be like our fear of the surgeon's knife, which must wound before it can heal. While we would prefer to forgo the pain altogether — or at the very least to perform our own surgery, thank you very much — our survival of the terrors depends on our trust in the surgeon's skill. If we believe the one to whom we surrender ourselves is competent, then, in the words of Julian of Norwich, all shall be well, and all shall be well, and all manner of things shall be well.

If we are open to this possibility in our interpretation of the Scripture, then we open the possibility of its being true in the interpretation of our lives as well. Whether the terror is heard on Sunday or lived on Monday, the hermeneutical question remains the same: do we trust God to act in all the events of our lives or only in the ones that meet with our approval?

Several summers ago I spent three days on a barrier island where loggerhead turtles were laying their eggs. One night while the tide was out, I watched a huge female heave herself up on the beach to dig her nest and empty herself into it while slow, salt tears ran from her eyes. Afraid of disturbing her, I left before she had finished her work but returned next morning to see if I could find the spot where her eggs lay hidden in the sand. What I found were her tracks, only they led in the wrong direction. Instead of heading back out to sea, she had wandered into the dunes, which were already hot as asphalt in the morning sun.

A little ways inland I found her, exhausted and all but baked, her head and flippers caked with dried sand. After pouring water on her and covering her with sea oats, I fetched a park ranger, who returned with a jeep to rescue her. As I watched in horror, he flipped her over on her back, wrapped tire chains around her front legs, and hooked the chains to the trailer hitch on his jeep. Then he took off, yanking her body forward so that her mouth filled with sand and then disappeared underneath her as her neck bent so far I feared it would break.

The ranger hauled her over the dunes and down onto the beach; I followed the path that the prow of her shell cut in the sand. At the ocean's edge, he unhooked her and turned her right side up again. She lay motionless in the surf as the water lapped at her body, washing the sand from her eyes and making her skin shine again. Then a particularly large wave broke over her, and she lifted her head slightly, moving her back legs as she did. As I watched, she revived. Every fresh wave brought her life back to her until one of them made her light enough to find a foothold and push off, back into water that was her home. Watching her swim slowly away and remembering her nightmare ride through the dunes, I noted that it is sometimes hard to tell whether you are being killed or saved by the hands that turn your life upside down.

Our hope, through all our own terrors, is that we are being saved. To hope this does not mean we lie down before the terrors, however. For as long as we have strength to fight, it is both our nature and our privilege to do so. Sometimes God's blessing does not come until daybreak, after a full night of wrestling angels, and sometimes it takes much longer than that. As preachers and as believers, it is our job to struggle with the terrors, refusing to let go of them until they have yielded their blessings.

The common lectionary's readings for Lent give us ample opportunity to explore both our struggle and our salvation. During the five weeks of Lent, the Old Testament lessons rehearse the history of God's covenant with humankind, beginning with the recital of that history in Deuteronomy 26 and continuing with God's promises to Abraham, Moses, Joshua, and Isaiah. These solid stories of relationship give us the ballast we need to survive the stormy blast of the Gospel lessons, which begin with Christ's severe testing in the wilderness before moving on to our own. "Lord," someone asks him in the lection for week two, "will only a few be saved?" (Luke 13:22). His answer is a stern yes, which he repeats in week three: "Unless you repent, you will all perish just as they did" (Luke 13:5).

Lent is the season to confront such terrifying news, not by buck-ling before it but by using its harsh light to examine the truth of our situation before God. It is a season to see through all our illusions about what will save us and to know for certain what will not. To use Jonathan Edwards's image, it is a time to abandon the twigs we have been using to keep us afloat and to reach out for the only raft that can bear our weight. Because the Good News means to change us, we inevitably hear it as bad news first. Is that harsh light really necessary? Couldn't I hang on to one medium-sized branch and sort of dog-paddle my way to shore? The gospel's answers this Lent are, respectively, yes and no. God does not mean to improve us but to save us, even if it scares us to death.

In week four, the story of the prodigal son shows us how it is done. Cashing in his relationship with his father, he journeys to a far coun-try where he loses all his twigs — money, pleasure, independence, adventure — none of them keeps him afloat, and soon he is floun-dering for his life, swimming back toward the shore of his father's embrace. He is dead when he arrives, but his father's love revives him. He was lost, and is found. The terrors do not overcome him, but they scare him to death, death that his father's open arms turn back into life.

In week five, death is no longer figurative but actual fact. Jesus visits the home of Lazarus, whom he has raised from the dead, and there Mary anoints him for his own burial. His death is inevitable, which is the chief terror of the gospel. Here is the best man God ever made, who has done nothing but right all his life, and what is his reward? Not ripe old age with grandchildren hanging on his sleeves but early, violent death on a cross. This death ruins all our efforts to turn the Bible into a manual for The Good Life. No one who has heard the story of Jesus Christ can mistake where following him will lead, which makes the gospel itself a text of terror for all who wish to avoid suf-fering and death. The Good News of God in Christ is heard loudest and best by those who stand on the far side of their own fresh graves.

On Palm Sunday we go through Luke's account of Christ's death in excruciating detail, as we will go through it again with John on Good Friday, but in between those two tombstones death recedes, looming above the narratives of Holy Week like a vulture in a tree. Meanwhile, Jesus enters Jerusalem to settle his affairs, speaking to the crowd for the last time and then withdrawing with his disciples, to instruct them and wash their feet.

All but one of the Gospel lessons for Holy Week are from John, which means that Jesus moves toward his death with a strong, prescient confidence. His life is not taken from him; he gives it willingly. If he is terrified, it does not show. Of all human beings, he is the most able to wade into the bloody darkness alone, trusting that he will not be alone forever or for long. In the background, the Old Testament lessons play the servant songs of Isaiah, reminding us that suffering has always been the vocation of God's chosen ones.

On Good Friday there is no escape. The vultures are perched low now; friends have vanished and the enemy is everywhere. The only good news is that there is one man who does not dissemble, one man who continues to speak the truth although it brings all the empires of this world crashing down on his head. According to John, Jesus does not give up his ghost until he knows that "It is finished" (19:30). Whether or not he knows what happens next, he knows that he is part of something beyond himself, something he has brought to fullness by surrendering himself to it as to the incalculable, incomparable will of God.

In faith, we believe that the terrors of Lent and of our lives are purifying terrors, confounding clauses in a covenant we may nonetheless trust. While they are washing all our certainties away, it is hard to believe they may also be cleansing us of our illusions, but that is the dare. If we are tempted to draw back from it and seek an easier way, we are not alone. The world is full of former disciples. "Do you also wish to go away?" Jesus asks the handful who are left him in the sixth chapter of John (6:67). "Lord," Simon Peter answers him, "to whom can we go? You have the words of eternal life."

8

PREACHING INTO THE NEXT MILLENNIUM

Barbara Brown Taylor

A New World Map

The next millennium is almost here. In no time at all we will be heading into Easter Sunday 2000, and on one hand it is nothing, a mere coincidence of zeros. But on the other hand it is something, if only a symbol for the great shift going on all around us. It is evident in nature, in politics, in science, in religion. It is evident in human consciousness, which may be the cause of these other changes but may just as well be the effect of them. Literally and figuratively, our maps are outdated. The world does not work the way we thought it did.

Until very recently, we believed in a world that could be understood and managed. We based that assumption on the work of Sir Isaac Newton, who wrote a startling book called *Principia* in 1686. In it, he suggested that the earth circled the sun, not vice versa, and that the atom was the basic building block of the universe. So far, so good. He also suggested that the solar system worked like a vast machine, in which both atom and planet obeyed identical laws. Summing up those laws in four simple algebraic formulas, he put the mystery of the universe to bed, where it stayed tucked in for the next four hundred years.

Believing he told us the truth about how the world worked, we modeled our nations, our economies, our families, and ourselves upon atomistic principles. You were you and I was I. If each of us would do our jobs, then the big machine should keep right on humming. According to our instruction manual, its operation was predictable. If something went wrong, you had only to break it down, find the defective part, and put it back together again. God was removed from the world, which could be explained without deity. Human beings were removed from the world as well. We no longer lived in it; we lived on it. It became an object to be used to our advantage, we who believed in a universe of manageable things.

During our lifetimes, this paradigm has come undone. The covers have come untucked, and mystery is once again loose in the cosmos. With the development of quantum physics, we discovered a subatomic world that did not behave the way Newton said it should. It was impossible to pin down, with waves turning into particles and particles into waves. What had mass one moment was pure energy the next, and none of it was predictable. The very act of observing a particle changed its behavior, which destroyed the whole notion of scientific objectivity. A scientist could not stand outside the world to watch it. The same particles that were busy responding to each other responded to the watcher as well, revealing a world that was not made up of manageable things but of constantly changing relationships.

It is no longer possible to think of the world as a machine. It behaves more like a living body, in which no part operates independently from the rest. The communication network of this body is still beyond anyone's grasp. In a discovery that upsets all our previous notions of space and time, we have found out that two particles separated by whole galaxies "know" what each other is doing. Change the spin on one and the other reverses its spin wherever it is — instantaneously — using some form of communication that is faster than light.

We think it has something to do with *field theory* — fields being invisible, nonmaterial structures that may turn out to be the basic substance of the universe. You know about gravitational fields and electromagnetic fields. Well, imagine another kind of field that knits the whole universe together — so that a shiver in the Milky Way gives us a shiver right here, faster than the speed of light.

Some of you are familiar with what is called the *butterfly effect*, first brought to our attention in 1961 by a research meteorologist named Edward Lorenz. Interested in why he could not come up with a foolproof forecast, he found that every weather pattern is acutely sensitive to the conditions present at its creation. When a butterfly beat its wings in Tokyo, he said, it affected the weather weeks later in New York. We are that connected. And yet we cannot say what the effect will be, exactly, since that is not possible in a dynamic, changing system like ours. All we can do is predict a range of possibilities and then wait to see what course the living system takes.

His discovery is an example of what we call *chaos theory*, which does not mean that reality is wildly out of control. It simply means that reality is essentially unpredictable because the world is an undivided whole and everything that happens one place in the web affects what is going on every place else in the web. There is an inherent order to the chaos — boundaries beyond which it will not go — but within those boundaries there are no observers, only participants.

Why am I telling you all this? Because it is changing the way we see the world, which means that it is changing us and the way we organize our life together, including church. Our politics are changing. Our economies are changing. The boundaries of our nations are changing, not to mention our minds. We are coming to the end of our love affair with finding out how things work. Knowing how to do things has not helped us decide whether or not we should do them. All our knowledge, all our technology, all our power, has not kept us from killing each other. It has not kept us from fouling our nest or forsaking our young. Something more is needed, something the universe seems to be trying to tell us about our connection with each other. We are one body. This is physics, not theology. Not that it matters. The God of one is the God of the other.

Millennial Whiplash

As the new science enters our consciousness, we are in for a shock. Our accustomed way of understanding the universe and our place in it has become outdated. Some historians say there has been nothing like it since the collapse of the Roman Empire. Everything we thought would save us has not. What we placed at the center of our lives has turned out to be toxic, and — as a culture anyway — we have not yet figured out what belongs there instead. In a kind of proverb for our times, biblical scholar Walter Brueggemann says, "The world for which you have been so carefully prepared is being taken away from you, by the grace of God." It is the last part that is the kicker, of course. The upheaval going on around us may be God's work, not the devil's. Our deadly way of life is collapsing in on itself, which we may read as punishment, evil, defeat. But it seems to me we may also read it as the beginning of redemption, as the deeply painful but necessary demolition that precedes new life.

Sometimes it is hard to tell the death throes from the labor pains, but as preachers that is our job: to help people sort them out, to preside at both the funeral and the birth, singing resurrection all the way. Each of us has all kinds of decisions to make about how we will address this changing world, not only as preachers and theologians but also as leaders of worship, administrators, pastors, and community representatives. The nature of our authority is changing, in case you had not noticed, along with the nature of our congregations. Whatever kind of church you serve, chances are you are preaching to a large number of people on antidepressants, to survivors of sexual abuse, to people who are addicted or recovering from addiction, to homosexual teenagers who contemplate suicide on a regular basis, to children in therapy for behavior disorders, as well as to people who come to church because they do not want to know about any of that and pray God will protect them from it as long as they live.

One thing I have noticed lately is the growing gap between the churched and the unchurched. I have been involved in a campus ministry this year that has brought me in contact with a wonderful, bright, funny group of college students who are positively phobic about church. They want to know why we have to call God *God*, why we cannot pray to Buddha along with Christ, why we do not take all the pews out of the church and sit in a circle on pillows instead.

And they are not the only ones. I also spend a good bit of time with people who have been away from the church for a long time and are flirting with coming back again, only there are certain things that bother them. They cannot, in good conscience, say the creed. "Our Father in heaven" strikes them as hopelessly archaic. They believe that the way we do church is harmful to their children, who will grow up thinking God wants them to sit still and be quiet. They want worship services and Sunday school curricula that celebrate the God of creative chaos and indeterminate gender.

And I do not disagree with them, but it is enough to give you whiplash, trying to comfort the frightened traditionalists with one hand while you are reaching out to the enlightened seekers with the other. It would be a whole lot easier to ignore one group or the other, which many churches have decided to do, but if you ask me, the stretch is an occupational hazard. It is just what you do when you are living between the end of one world and the beginning of the next.

To make it too simple, there are those who respond to a changing world by letting go of the past and those who respond by hanging on tighter. Most of our congregations include some of each, people who will continue to keep the issues fresh for us. How do we honor the tradition we have received from our ancestors without worshiping them instead of God? How do we declare what God has done without shutting ourselves down to what God may do next? "Do not remember the former things, or consider the things of old," thus said the Lord to Isaiah in the forty-third chapter of his book; "I am about to do a new thing; now it springs forth, do you not perceive it?" (vv. 18–19).

Implications for Preaching

If there is anything to the scenario I have described, then what are the implications for preaching? In a quantum world, the possibilities are endless, but I will limit myself to three — three movements I believe are in store both for us as preachers and for the people whom we serve. The first is the movement from individualism to community. The second is the movement from knowledge to passion. And the third is the movement from overfamiliarity to reverence. These are all modest proposals, based on my own limited experience and thinking. I offer them to you for fun.

First is the movement from individualism to community. If the new science is teaching us anything, it is that we are linked together in ways we do not even understand, and yet one thing I notice when I listen to sermons — including my own — is how often they treat a congregation like a collection of individuals, addressing individual behavior, individual faith, individual fears. The point, I suppose, is for each person to sense that he or she has been spoken to directly, and sometimes they will even say it at the door. "Have you been reading my mail? Preacher, you were really talking to me today."

This is meant to be a compliment, and it is fine, as far as it goes. A person comes to church from a life in the world, receives a dose of the divine, and goes back to that life in the world, which is likely to be competitive and somewhat fractured. This is because it is based on atomistic principles, which treat people like machines. Keep them tuned and oiled, and they do good work. If they break down, you can take them apart and put them back together again, or you can discard them for newer models. In an atomistic world, nothing is greater or less than the sum of its parts. One plus one always equals two, and one is the basic building block of the universe.

The church knows another reality, in which one plus one is the beginning of something beyond calculation and the basic building block of the universe is not one but "wherever two or three are gathered in my name" (Matt. 18:20). Or according to an old Sufi saying, "You think because you understand one you must also understand two, because one and one make two. But you must also understand and." Our business is relationship, which does not stop with relating individuals to God. Our good news is that God has related us to one another and that the least act of love has infinite consequences. We are one body, whether we act like it or not. We belong to one web that stretches across the universe, uniting us to all that is, seen and unseen. My true name is not "I" but "we." There is only one "I" in the world — the Great I Am — and even that one, we believe, is three. If you have no other use for the doctrine of the Trinity, this is enough: that even God exists in relationship.

So wouldn't it be interesting if someone came out of church on Sunday morning and said, "Preacher, you were really talking to us this morning"? What if we could, through our preaching, support that sense of belonging to a body that is more than its parts, that has a life and a purpose of its own, in which people do not feel like individual atoms but like members of a whole? A pluralistic whole, by the way, not a homogeneous one. Again, I cite the Trinity, which is the Christian church's genius metaphor for unity in diversity.

This shift of perspective will take place first in the mind of the preacher, who will begin to notice the personality of the congregation as something more than the personalities in the congregation. This may happen through as formal a process as congregational analysis, but it may also happen informally, by noticing the ratio between salads and desserts at potluck suppers, say, or by asking newcomers to give you their first impressions or by watching to see whether leaders work together or alone.

Based on what you see when you observe these things, you may begin to offer the congregation images of themselves in community —

not a collection of individuals but a body with a word to say and a job to do. This will go beyond their own local identity. Preachers may also deepen the congregation's sense of community by telling stories from other communities, by which I mean not only other ethnic, religious, and socioeconomic communities but also other communities of discourse. How long has it been since you preached a sermon that engaged the scientific community or the business community or the community of the arts? Their language may be different from ours, but God is busy in all those communities, and to make connections between what they are doing and what we are doing can provide a heady sense of wholeness. When we do the opposite — when our sermons are full of churchy talk about churchy things — I think we increase our isolation, giving people the impression that religion is something separate from the rest of their lives.

Next I want to address the movement from knowledge to passion. I have read two good books on preaching lately. One is *Speaking from the Heart* by Richard Ward, and the other is *With Ears to Hear* by Robin Meyers. Both make a similar point: that the only preacher worth listening to is one who is passionately involved in his or her message. If you do not think of yourself as an especially passionate person, this may sound like bad news to you, but take heart. What they are both saying, I think, is that the first step toward preaching a lively word is living it. Or, as Fred Craddock put it a long time ago, "Appropriation of the gospel is the minimum condition for standing in the pulpit."

Without denigrating the value of biblical and theological knowledge, I want to suggest that it is no longer enough. It may never have been enough, but in our late-twentieth-century age of information saturation, knowledge can become just one more addiction. We are hunting something more visceral than that, something with power to sustain and direct our lives. You know it when you hear it. Someone stands up to preach, and the first thing you notice is that it is a real voice, not a phony one. This is not someone doing an imitation of a preacher. This is someone speaking to you from the heart, in the same voice he would use to wish you happy birthday or say a prayer by your bed. No high drama, no polished gestures, but gravity, yes — the unmistakable sense that what he is about to say matters, to him and to you. You may even get the sense that it has cost him something — some sleep, some peace of mind — that putting this sermon together has required more of him than working a crossword puzzle or washing the car.

I believe that the best thing we can do for our preaching is to surrender ourselves to God and our neighbors and then to tell the truth about what that is like. It is so important not to lie. We do so much damage when we tell people things are easier than they are or that if they just do this, then that will happen or God will make everything all right. They want to believe us, but they know better, and the net effect is that they learn to keep us separate from the rest of their lives. They nod at our sweet lies on Sunday, and on Monday they go back to surviving anyway they can.

The more we ground our sermons in everyday life, the better. The more we tell the truth about human experience, the better. And the more we avoid religious cliché, the better.

Three weeks ago at the airport I was waiting for my luggage when I heard a couple talking behind me.

"How was your flight?" he said.

"It was awful!" she said. "I had to sit next to an [expletive deleted] preacher, and you know how they are. Yakety-yakety-yak, the whole way. I got everything — God, Jesus, the Bible — everything. They've got no-smoking flights. Next time I'm going to ask for a no-preaching flight."

I am afraid I know what she meant, and preachers are not the only ones who suffer from it. It is a disconnection from true life, a disconnection from true feeling, that so often turns our talk into yakety-yakety-yak, that and a disconnection from each other that keeps us from listening. *Passion*, I think, is one word for recovering the connections — between you and me, between God and us, between us and the whole creation — preaching that comes from the heart and the gut as well as the mind, describing a life that is recognizable to our hearers, a world they live in. If they cannot trust us to speak the truth about earthly things, how then will they trust us when we come to the heavenly ones?

In the next millennium, knowledge *about* God will not preach. Knowledge *of* God will. And if that is too much to ask, then passionate pursuit of God will do. Those who listen to us expect more than a history lesson on Luke-Acts plus some freeze-dried stories we got out of a book. They want food for their hearts. They want help for their souls. They want to see Jesus, or at least someone who knows Jesus, and God help us if we offer them less than that.

The last movement I want to talk about is the movement from overfamiliarity to reverence for God. The new science has taught us that we do not know as much as we thought we knew. There is coherence to the universe we may never understand and mystery that goes way, way deeper than the stars. At home by my bed I have a book called *The Physics of Immortality*. In it, Tulane cosmologist Frank Tipler declares that — quite by accident — science led him straight to God. He is not the only one who has said so, which is, frankly, awesome. Science and theology have been divorced since the seventeenth century, when Newton suggested that math, not God, ran the universe. Now mathematical physicists are telling us it just is not so, and a rapprochement is underway.

What is going on is a reunion of cosmic proportions. Science and theology have traveled so far away from each other that they are coming back together again, and we are lucky enough to see it happening. Historian Morris Berman calls it the "re-enchantment of the world," or at least that is what he hopes it is — a return to what we knew before the scientific revolution persuaded us we did not, namely, that we are part of a cosmos we are not in charge of, a living system that invites us to participate, not dominate. Dominion belongs to God alone.

I do not know how all of this affects you, but it makes me think we have gotten a little too chummy with God. Tune in to many of our churches on Sunday mornings, and you will hear preachers speaking of God as they would speak of a pet lion — oh, he was fierce once, but there is nothing to be afraid of now. You can climb on his back if you want to. We've had all his teeth and claws pulled, so he can't hurt you anymore.

If you do not know Annie Dillard's work, you should. There is a fine passage in her book *Teaching a Stone to Talk* about how blithely we invoke the power of God. "It is madness to wear ladies' straw hats and velvet hats to church," she writes; "we should all be wearing crash helmets. Ushers should issue life preservers and signal flares; they should lash us to our pews. For the sleeping god may awake someday and take offense, or the waking god may draw us out to where we can never return." She goes on to tell the story of the Hasidic rabbi who refused to promise a friend he would visit the next day. "How could you ask me to make such a promise?" he asked his friend. "This evening I must pray and recite, 'Hear, O Israel, the Lord our God, the Lord is One.' When I say these words, my soul goes out to the utmost rim of life. . . . Perhaps I shall not die this time either, but how can I now promise to do something . . . after the prayer?"[1]

How long has it been since you worried about dying at your prayers? Not because your cholesterol finally got you but because God heard you and came to meet you face-to-face? It has been a long time for me, but I am at least smarter than my friends who are always telling God they are ready for anything God wants them to do. "O God," I pray, "I know you have lots of other things to do, so it's fine with me if you want to move me down your list. I've got plenty to do here, more than enough, really, and I'm not sure I'm up to a direct encounter."

I have read my Bible. I know what happens to people who see God face-to-face, and it seems to me that we are a little short on reverence these days. We say God's name out loud without even bowing. We talk about what God thinks and wants as if we knew what that was. We speak of God's love as if it were all soft pillows when it is more like bone-melting thunder. "Love in action," says Father Zosima in Dostoyevsky's *The Brothers Karamazov*, "is a harsh and dreadful thing, compared with love in dreams."

Again, this shift will take place first in the mind of the preacher, whose reverence for God may lead her to say less, not more, about God's ultimate being and doing. Robert Farrar Capon uses an apt metaphor in this regard. When we try to describe God, he says, we are like oysters trying to describe a ballerina.[2] In the end, we may only be able to describe what we love, substituting psalms for expositions.

The next millennium is less than four years away. By chance or by plan, it coincides with a major shift in human consciousness. As treasurers of God's Word, we have the very great privilege of deciding how we will respond to that shift — or more pertinently, how we will take part in it — by perceiving and proclaiming the new things God is doing in our sight.

---

1. Annie Dillard, *Teaching a Stone to Talk* (New York: Harper & Row, 1982), 40–41.
2. Robert Farrar Capon, *Hunting the Divine Fox* (Minneapolis: Winston Press, 1985), 7–8.

9

THE EASTER SERMON

Barbara Brown Taylor

If preachers' knees get weak at the thought of Easter Sunday, it is not only the burden of doing justice to the resurrection. It is also the cultural and emotional weight of the day. Easter Sunday is the day we celebrate the central mystery of Christian faith. It is also the day the children come dressed like sugar confections, flanked by grandparents flown in from Idaho and Maine. It is the day the flower guild outdoes itself, the day the choir has anticipated for months. It is the day of the annual Easter egg hunt, the day the cooks in the congregation keep looking at their watches. It is the day everyone is supposed to be happy, lovely, and well-fed, which is somewhat at odds with the gospel.

Last year on Palm Sunday, tornadoes ripped through northeast Georgia. Homes and businesses were lifted off their foundations; pine forests were flattened; whole barns full of chickens were sucked up and swept away. The news from Alabama was worse, where workers pulled bodies from the ruins of a church. No one said it out loud, but it seemed the worst kind of betrayal on God's part. If anyone in the world should have been spared destruction, surely it was believers gathered for worship in God's house.

Where I live, the nightmare continued through Holy Week. People woke screaming from their sleep. Chain saws roared through the day and into the night. Local shelters pleaded for food, water, and clothes. I listened to one woman tell me what it was like to be woken from her Sunday afternoon nap by the sound of a locomotive wind tearing trees from their roots. She was eight-months pregnant with her first child at the time and was sure they both would die. She had never known terror like that, she said, a panic so deep it would last for months, triggered by the least blow of wind. But she did not die. Every tree on her wooded lot was bent, broken, or gone, but her house survived. Surveying the mess on Maundy Thursday, she put her hands on her hips. "Well," she said, "I always wanted a meadow."

I thought of her when it came time to write the Easter sermon. I thought of everyone who had literally been scared to — or by — death. I thought of the Alabama mother burying her child, the church members burying their dreams of safety, everyone whose trust in God had been dealt a body blow that Palm Sunday afternoon, and I wondered: Does this ruin Easter? Or is this what Easter is all about?

One thing that occurs to me is that we have a hard time celebrating Easter properly because we are wholly unwilling to die first. If anything, we are tempted to celebrate Easter as a festive denial of death — the day on which everyone is supposed to be happy, lovely, and well-fed. Faith in God means we do not have to worry about death. Jesus has taken care of it. Jesus will take care of it. All we have to do is believe.

Some religious art supports this temptation. I remember studying one altar panel — was it Grünewald — in which the risen Christ floated above his vacant tomb. He was dressed in flowing white and blue robes. His face was clean; his hair was neat; his hands and eyes were upraised in gratitude. His feet did not touch the ground; they were socked in a white cloud that separated him from everything on earth.

Years later I saw another version of the same event. In it a gaunt, wounded man stumbled from the black mouth of his grave wearing nothing but a strip of linen around his loins. His bare feet were on the ground. His hurt places looked like they still hurt. He clearly needed something to eat, but there was such a look of stunned triumph on his face that I had no doubt he would live. I also had no doubt he had been dead. He had returned from some place so far and beyond this world that only God could have brought him back. It was not a rescue; it was a resurrection, and he looked like it had cost him plenty.

No one will ever know how he really looked, of course, because no one was there to see. The crucifixion was the public event, the one with all the eyewitnesses. The resurrection took place in private — a choice made by God that preachers might do well to respect. We can say too much about what we do not know for sure, violating the essential mystery of what happened between father and son that morning.

Like the others who followed the crucified one, we were not invited to his resurrection. All we have ever been given to consider are an open grave and some linen rags lying around — that and the dreamlike accounts of those who saw him later.

Maybe that is why Good Friday rings truer in some believers' hearts than Easter Sunday. Good Friday is verifiable, then and now. It is where we live, in the land of betrayal, corruption, violence, and death. Easter is a rumor by comparison. Someone said that someone saw him, only it didn't look like him, exactly, and before anyone could believe it was him, he was gone. After Easter, he comes and goes like a rainbow on a bright day: now you see him; now you don't. Didn't our hearts burn within us while he talked to us on the road? It is the best kind of rumor, but one we can only test by dying ourselves.

Butterflies are popular symbols of resurrection, the idea being that a fuzzy caterpillar spins a sleeping bag around itself and emerges sometime later as a glorious new creature. The reality is somewhat more gruesome. If you slice open a cocoon early in this process, you will not find a sleeping caterpillar with tiny wing buds on its back. You will find a bag of mush because the caterpillar must utterly disintegrate before the butterfly can begin. The change is not a gentle, aesthetic one. It is radical and complete. The birth of the new creature requires the annihilation of the old.

Preachers who would like more coaching in this easy-to-say, hard-to-grasp equation may read Robert Farrar Capon's *Parables of Grace*. In Capon's view, death is all we can know of resurrection for now. The rest is faith, and all our efforts to resist death amount to our refusal of God's grace. "He will not take our cluttered life, as we hold it, into eternity," Capon says. "He will take only the clean emptiness of our death in the power of Jesus' resurrection."[1]

Another fine resource for Easter is Reynolds Price's autobiographical work, *A Whole New Life*. Ten years after his diagnosis of spinal cancer — years of struggling to save his life the way he knew it — he says it would have been a great favor to him if someone had walked up to his hospital bed right at the start and said, "Reynolds Price is dead. Who will you be now?"

---

1. Robert Farrar Capon, *Parables of Grace* (Grand Rapids: Eerdmans, 1988), 182.

That person is dead as any teen-aged Marine drilled through the forehead in an Asian jungle; any Navy Seal with his legs blown off, halved for the rest of the time he gets; any woman mangled in her tenderest parts, unwived, unmothered, unlovered and shorn. Have one hard cry, if the tears will come. Then stanch the grief, by whatever legal means. Next find your way to be somebody else, the next viable you — a stripped-down whole other clear-eyed person, realistic as a sawed-off shotgun and thankful for air, not to speak of the human kindness you'll meet if you get normal luck.[2]

I am not sure how you preach this sort of thing without getting crucified yourself. We hear a lot these days about the postmodern church, the idea being that Christendom is over and we can no longer behave in our old triumphal ways, but that is hard to tell in most churches on Easter morning. We work hard to celebrate the way we have always celebrated, even if that means setting our clocks back forty years, and part of the old triumphal message is that death cannot touch those who believe. To say anything else is to go up against the icon of Easter morning. To speak of the absolute necessity of death may strike some as profoundly distasteful, like speaking of Mary's contractions on Christmas Eve.

Easter vigil services offer preachers on this theme a better chance to be heard. A properly held vigil begins in a dark, cold, empty church — a tomb, in other words. With the lighting of the Paschal fire a small dawn begins to break; only the world does not know it yet. The first hour of the service is held by candlelight, with believers sitting in the dark listening to all the old stories — the flood, the sacrifice of Isaac, the escape from Egypt, the valley of dry bones. These are triumphal stories, but they are also full of death — the complete surrender of the known world in exchange for a new one of God's own making.

Then comes the baptismal covenant with its renewal of baptismal vows. If no one is being initiated at the vigil, it is still a good idea to have water on hand. Dip a branch of cedar in it and fling fragrant water on those present, reminding them of their own death and resurrection as members of Christ's body. Watch them flinch at first and then relax. Watch smiles creep over some of their faces. This can

---

2. Reynolds Price, *A Whole New Life* (New York: Atheneum, 1994), 183.

seem to last forever, this waiting in the dark, but when dawn breaks and someone shouts, "Alleluia, Christ is risen!" your heart can pound like you have rolled away the stone all by yourself.

The difference between the vigil service and the principal services of Easter morning has always struck me as the difference between the first-century church and the church of Constantine. At 8:00 a.m. I climb out of the catacombs and into the cathedral, where the banners are flapping and the trumpets are tuning up. It is helpful at this point to remember that I am a very small part of this ancient drama. All the fanfare suggests that my sermon must be huge, but it is not so. My job is more like that of the person who offers the toast at a wedding reception. The wedding is the point. My job is to address it as respectfully and succinctly as I can.

This is often a matter of simply telling the truth. There may be no better service a preacher can render on Easter morning than to resist hyperbole and fly close to the ground, saying the bare minimum about what we can know and what we cannot, about where knowing runs out and faith begins, about what is our business and what belongs to God alone. I recently read a book review in which the author was praised for "leaving all the right things unsaid so that the silence resounds," and it occurred to me that we could use more silence in our sermons these days. By *silence* I do not mean the literal absence of speech, although that might not be a bad idea. I mean fewer, more carefully chosen words, with less presumption in them. I mean greater respect for the mystery of God, which passes all understanding, and deeper humility about our own relative size in the universe.

We live in a close-up age of engagement. The evening news brings us face-to-face with victims around the world. Televised trials turn us into jury and judge. Radio talk shows urge us to air our opinions. If we want to look at the rings of Saturn, we can. If we want to look at a strand of DNA, we can. Intimacy with our universe is a given. We invade each other's privacy as a matter of course, and we do not seem to stop when we come to God. We approach the Almighty like investigative reporters, speculating about things we can never know, like whose side God is on and when the world will end and why terrible things happen to faithful people. We have misplaced our sense of awe — our appropriate fear — of a God of enormous privacy. In the words of the prophet Jeremiah, we do not know how to blush (8:12).

In the temple in Jerusalem, in the old days, the inner sanctuary was known as the holy of holies, a place so charged with the divine presence that only the high priest could enter it. The room itself was empty except for a throne, which was also empty. Two gold cherubim spread their wings over it, facing each other across the mercy seat. Once a year their solitude was broken — when the high priest came to make amends for the people on the Day of Atonement. Inside that room, he had only one job: to utter the sacred name of God. The problem was, it was all vowels consonants, and without vowels no one knew how to pronounce it. No one was allowed to try, for that matter, but as the high priest breathed in and out, he could hear the sacred name on his lips. Yah-weh. I am who I am. I will be who I will be. God's perfect freedom, confessed with every human breath.

According to Lawrence Kushner, who tells this story, "Creation has at its center an empty throne in an empty room in which the unpronounceable Name is spoken once a year. And the sound of its name is the sound of breathing!"[3] He adds a pungent detail to the story. Before the high priest goes into the presence of the Lord, the other priests tie a rope around his leg so that if he is struck dead inside, they can haul him out without risking destruction themselves.

We, meanwhile, crawl right into God's lap and start asking, "Why?" Perhaps Jesus himself has emboldened us, calling God "Abba" and telling us not to fear. There is still room for reverence. There are still times to leave all the right things unsaid so that the silence resounds.

The Gospels teach us what those things are. For Easter Day there are two choices: Luke at the vigil and Luke or John at the principal service. As different as they are, there is a central emptiness to them both. In Luke, the resurrection proclamation is not about Christ's presence but about his absence. "He is not here," say the two men in dazzling clothes (24:5). In John, it is Mary who names both his absence and the limits of her understanding: "They have taken the Lord out of the tomb and we do not know where they have laid him" (20:2). This is how Easter dawns in the human heart. He is not here. We do not know where he is. The tomb is as empty as the throne in

---

3. Lawrence Kushner, *GOD was in this PLACE & I, i did not know* (Woodstock, Vt.: Jewish Lights, 1991), 97.

the holy of holies, and the sound of God's name is the sound of our own ragged breath.

Preachers who wish to say more than this may do so at their own risk. It would not be a bad idea to have someone tie a rope around your leg first. On this one day a year, we go as near the mystery as we dare, only we must surrender all our presumption at the door. Great reverence is called for, great silence before the ineffable power and privacy of God. Our best words turn to ash in the presence of the resurrection, and yet we are called to try, to keep reaching for ways to say what God has done.

In his *Four Quartets*, T. S. Eliot confesses his twenty-year struggle with words, words that come to him too late.

> ...And so each venture
> is a new beginning, a raid on the inarticulate
> With shabby equipment always deteriorating
> In the general mess of imprecision of feeling,
> Undisciplined squads of emotion. And what there is to conquer
> By strength and submission, has already been discovered
> Once or twice, or several times, by men whom one cannot hope
> To emulate — but there is no competition —
> There is only the fight to recover what has been lost
> And found and lost again and again: and now, under conditions
> That seem unpropitious. But perhaps neither gain nor loss.
> For us, there is only the trying. The rest is not our business.[4]

---

4. T. S. Eliot, *Four Quartets* (New York: Harcourt Brace, 1971), 31.

10

POSTMODERN PREACHING
Learning to Love the Thickness of the Text

WILLIAM H. WILLIMON

Last summer I attempted to read the Koran, the holy book of Moslems. After all, we are having an increasing number of Moslems on campus, and what better way to understand a faith than to read its texts? For starters I discovered that one cannot really read the Koran in English. There are English translations, to be sure, but none of these is recognized as scripture. The only true Koran is in Arabic. One must learn Arabic in order to read the true Koran. Odd that Christians have not put similar linguistic restraints upon the reading of our texts.

Despite my earnest efforts, I didn't make it through the Koran. For one thing, Mohammed got on my nerves. Mohammed, the prophet of the one true God, has an opinion on everything: how to weigh grain, how to cut meat, homosexuality (he is against it). I bogged down in the eight pages or so on women during their menstrual cycles. It really is amazing how many issues there are in which Jesus appears to have had absolutely no interest. And we can all be thankful for that.

For another thing, Mohammed never tells stories. Ask him a question, he gives you a straight answer. "I have three things I want to say about how to run a government...," he will say. Quite a contrast with Jesus' telling Peter to go get tax money out of the mouth of a fish. Mohammed always answers every question. Jesus, almost never. The Koran has a low tolerance for ambiguity, narrative, enigma; the Bible wallows in it.

When one reads the Koran, one knows immediately why there

are "Moslem fundamentalists."[1] Yet it is more difficult to understand why there are those who read say, the Gospel of Luke, and find therein "fundamentals." Luke is "thick"; the literature is polyvalent, predominantly narrative, almost never propositional, open to multiple interpretations, defying reductionistic reading. In fact, after a few weeks into the Koran, switching back to Luke, the reader is apt to feel that the biblical texts are almost intentionally obscure, more difficult and strange than they need to be.[2] The thick, impenetrable nature of these texts may be by conscious design. A hard to understand text catches our attention, begs for attention, engages our natural human inclination to figure things out. On the other hand, the texts may be difficult, obscure, and distant simply because they are talking about what is true whereas most of what we live is false. A living, righteous, prickly God tends to produce difficult Scripture.[3]

For instance, this Easter many of us will struggle with John 20. John first does the story of Easter as a footrace between the disciples in which they came, then they "saw and believed" (John 20:8). Believed what? John says that "as yet they did not understand the scripture, that he must rise from the dead" (20:9). Presumably, they believed that the body had been stolen. Or maybe they believed something else, such as the return of the robin in the spring or the emergence of the butterfly from the cocoon. At any rate, whatever they believed was not yet quite Easter. Easter ends with everyone going back home (20:10), and that was that. At least the *men* go home. Mary stays behind to weep. She is confronted by the risen Christ, whom she regards as either the gardener or a body snatcher, or perhaps both (20:15).

---

1. The term "Moslem fundamentalists" appears to be a creation of the Western press to explain why there are some people who take their religion very seriously in a world (the West) where most of us do not. *All* Moslems interpret their texts in ways that the West might label as "fundamentalist." My point here is that the texts themselves beg for this sort of reading.

2. I suppose it was Wittgenstein who was among the first moderns to notice that biblical texts appear to be almost intentionally opaque. Why is it that the biblical authors want to communicate yet also want to be difficult? Might it be that the authors want to do something to the texts' readers (hearers) through the very difficulty of the texts? Ludwig Wittgenstein, *Culture and Value*, ed. G. H. Von Wright, trans. Peter Winch (Oxford: Basil Blackwell, 1980).

3. Luther delightfully complains about the prophets who, to the father of the modern German language, have "a queer way of talking, like people who, instead of proceeding in an orderly manner, ramble off from one thing to the next, so that you cannot make head or tail of them or see what they are getting at." Quoted in Gerhard von Rad, *The Message of the Prophets* (New York: Harper & Row, 1967), 15.

Then, just to keep things interesting, John 20:19 begins Easter all over again with the story of Thomas and his doubts. Defying resolution or simple understanding, the risen Christ appears again in John 21 in a complex, utterly enigmatic appearance, which becomes quite convoluted with details of fish, fishing nets, Peter, and feeding sheep.

We have a "problem" with this literature. Our problem is not, as we sometimes flatter ourselves into believing, that we are modern, critical, and skeptical whereas the text is naive, primitive, and credulous. That was historical-criticism's reading of our interpretive dilemma. Fortunately, we now know what simplistic, reductionistic, and historically naive readings historical criticism rendered.[4]

No, I have come to believe that our problem is that we have become tone-deaf to a text so thick, so opaque, so rich, as John 20–21. We are ill-equipped to hear the Easter text. After all, we are modern, Western folk who have taught ourselves to be content with a flat, well-defined, and utterly accessible world. Our world has become "user friendly," for we can imagine no world worth having that is not subject to our utility. Our ways of knowing are positivistic, historicist, and inherently reductionistic.[5]

In thinking about Easter, Bishop John Spong asked a public-radio interviewer, "How can my daughter, who is earning her Ph.D. in physics, possibly be asked to believe in the bodily resurrection of Jesus?" The answer, I suppose, depends on Spong's daughter. I have known some rather simpleminded physicists in my time. How little imagination does his daughter now have? Perhaps the story John has to tell is now utterly inaccessible to her. Perhaps, on the other hand, with training and time, she could learn that there is a world that is as-yet undreamed of in her philosophy. The text cannot be blamed if modern people (of whom Bishop Spong is among the last holdouts) live by epistemologies too limited to enable them to hear the text.

---

4. See Walter Brueggemann's wonderful "Preaching as Reimagination," *Theology Today* (October 1995): 313–29, for a wonderfully concise rendering of his continuing quarrel with historical criticism.

5. In his now notorious defense of historical criticism in *The Interpreter's Dictionary of the Bible* (Nashville: Abingdon Press, 1962), 1:431, Krister Stendahl contended that we preachers must answer to the objective, dispassionate, honest work of the not-necessarily-believing-anything "descriptive biblical theologian." Fortunately, James Sanders corrected Stendahl's hermeneutical naïveté in his article "Hermeneutics" in *The Interpreter's Dictionary of the Bible: The Supplementary Volume* (Nashville: Abingdon Press, 1976), 402–7, in which Sanders drops the pretense to scientific objectivity, urging us to approach the text with humility and humor.

Robert Alter says that, until the parables of Kafka or James Joyce's *Ulysses*, there is a sense in which we modern people had lost the skills necessary to read the Bible. Only after artists were again determined to write reality on a number of levels, exploring the complexities of human consciousness, the mystery of time, the polyvalence of words, were we able to ask the right questions of 1 Kings.[6]

William C. Placher makes the evocative suggestion that the very messiness of the biblical texts — the way they parallel each other, conflict, repeat, fail to connect — is an embodiment of the God which they try to bring to speech: "The narratives of this God who eschews brute force were not edited with the brute force necessary to impose a single, clear framework."[7] Just as this God, according to a number of the parables of Jesus, is willing to live with wasted seed, a net full of good and bad fish, and a garden where the weeds mix with the wheat, eschewing violent, coercive purification and harmonizing, so the willingness of the biblical writers and canonizers to live with the messiness of the texts is a testimonial to their faith in a God who chooses to suffer, to embrace human messiness, and to love us in our inconsistency rather than to force us to make sense.

I recently said to a friend who is an expert on Russia, "Things have really become messy over there since the demise of the Soviet Union, what with the breakaway republics, the rebellions, and difficulties." He replied, "No. Things were always messy, interesting, and conflicted there, though for a time Soviet tanks made it seem unified and coherent."

The modern lust for unity, for a center, for coherence and cohesiveness, produced not only perhaps the most violent century the world has ever known but also some of the most dreary centralized governments and collectivist schemes, to say nothing of some of the ugliest architecture the world has ever known. Any century that admires New York's World Trade Center or the Atlanta Airport will find John 20–21 to be tough going.

The interpretive skills that many of us learned in seminary invari-

---

6. Here I commend Susan Handelman's *The Slayers of Moses* (Albany, N.Y.: State University of New York Press, 1982). Handelman praises the traditional rabbinical methods of biblical interpretation, which relished the endlessness of interpretive possibilities and which loved certain biblical texts precisely because they were so impervious to "right" readings.

7. William C. Placher, *Narratives of a Vulnerable God: Christ, Theology, and Scripture* (Louisville: Westminster/John Knox, 1995), 88.

ably took a superior stance toward the text; modernity is inherently arrogant. We have been conditioned to feel that we moderns are privileged to stand at the summit of human development, uniquely equipped to stand in judgment upon any idea or anyone who preceded us. All knowing is tied to some scheme of power, and in a capitalistic, democratic culture, all knowing begins and ends with the sovereign consumer. So we ask, "What does this text mean to me?" or, more precisely, "What can I *do* with this text?" before simply sitting quietly and letting the text have its way with us.

We cut apart the text, split it up into its smallest units, sever it from the community that produced it, lop off that which offends our modern sensibilities — my verbs are intentional. We are doing the same violence to the text that we do to any culture or people who are strange to us, who don't fit into the categories that we received from the Enlightenment, who refuse to produce the commodities we value.[8]

Much of our violence begins with our modern lust for the one "right" interpretation, the one official reading.[9] All interpretation, including historical criticism (*especially* historical criticism), serves some configuration of power, some social arrangement. I once thought it shameful that "uninformed" laypersons were busy interpreting biblical texts in all sorts of ways, without the benefit of academic training. I now honor such diversity of readings — particularly when they occur among folk who are not only seeking to understand the text but to embody and perform the text — as ecclesial resistance against the powers-that-be who serve the academy rather than the church.

What I am pleading for here is an interpretive approach to our Scripture that is true to the form of the Scripture itself. Just as the Koran, by its very form, renders certain kinds of readers, so the Bible,

---

8. Alas, much of the "hermeneutics of suspicion," particularly the type practiced by feminists like Elisabeth Schüssler Fiorenza (*In Memory of Her: A Feminist Theological Reconstruction of Christian Origins* [New York: Crossroad, 1983]), is not nearly suspicious enough of its own subservience to the epistemologies of the Enlightenment. A reductionistic reading of texts in favor of "liberation" or some other unifying prior principle can be an unwarranted coercion of the odd voice of the text. It is easier to see the cultural conditioning of the text than acknowledge our own.

9. Placher recalls the remarkable story of Bishop Theodoret's suppression (A.D. 423) of Tatian's *Diatessaron*. The book was Tatian's attempt to harmonize the four Gospels into one. Despite the way Theodoret went about it, the bishop was right in defending the diversity and difficulty of interpretation represented by our having four Gospels rather than one. *Narratives of a Vulnerable God*, 86–87.

by its form, is more congenial to certain interpretive strategies than to others.

So when a bright young student emerged from Duke Chapel complaining, "Your sermon today was hard to follow. It didn't seem well organized. What was the point?" I of course responded, "Well, I did better than Mark does. At least mine had a beginning and an end, which is more than you can say for his Gospel."

The text itself encourages and provokes uncentering, dislocation, and dislodgment. The very thickness of the text may be part of the text's strategic assault upon our received world.

I think we need to condition our people to expect interpretive difficulty on Sunday morning, to relish the multiplicity of messages, to love the thickness of the text, to come to church expecting to have their present reality subverted by the demanding text. Too many of us preachers say, after reading a troublesome text, "Give me twenty minutes, and I will explain this for you." Even to read a troublesome text and then to say, in a well-modulated voice, "Now I have three things I want to say about this," begins to defuse the text, make it make sense without allowing the text time to make us make sense. To be baptized is to be willing to let the text stand in a superior interpretive position to us, not the other way around. Rather than treating the text like a cadaver to be dissected, we ought to pray with the psalmist, "O LORD, thou has searched me, and known me" (Ps. 139:1 KJV).

This stress upon the plurality of meanings, the thickness of the text, the surplus of textual significance, may sound woefully relativistic and slippery, imagination out of control. Have we joined forces with the postmodernists who believe that there is no reality other than the text? We part company with Derrida and other postmodernists who seem to believe that there is only text (modernism is always asserting that things are *only* one thing or another), that there can be no external referent to the text.[10] We Christians really do believe that behind these texts stands the risen Christ, that these texts eventually render a living God who has graciously chosen to be revealed in these texts. To be a baptized Christian is to be someone who is busy believing that these seemingly disordered, often exasperating, sometimes

---

10. See Jacques Derrida, *Of Grammatology*, trans. Gayatri Chakravorty Spivak (Baltimore: Johns Hopkins University Press, 1976).

threatening, texts ultimately have portrayed the true God truthfully. In fact, over time, many of us come to believe that these texts are true to the living God of Israel precisely because they are so seemingly disordered, exasperating, and threatening.

Does this relativize interpretation, making all interpretations of Scripture equally valid? What about the objective truth of the text? Is it all as slippery and ill-defined as this? Even to ask such questions betrays our unwillingness to relax, to let down our defenses, and to let the text have its way with us. Where did we get the notion that truth must be "objectively true" or that truth ought not be "relative"? Where did we get the notion that it is possible for something not to be relative? Even to use the word *relative* is to assume that there is some freestanding, self-contained reality out there somewhere that has freed itself from the contingencies of history and relationship to anything other than itself. Modernity hoped to uncover objective truth by grounding its epistemology in a universal account of human rationality. Truth, to be true to modernity, had to be collectivist, large, unified, logical (as the Enlightenment defined logic), so logical that no thinking human being could resist it without being subhuman. Ours has been an age eager to label those who put forward other accounts of truth as "primitive," "tribalistic," "fanatical," or "subhuman." The gulag, Hitler's ovens, and the extermination of Native Americans were grounded in an epistemology that believed truth was universally, objectively valid.[11]

If you think that truth has to be consistent or universally valid or objectively true or some other nonbiblical definition of true, then you ought to go worship that definition of truth and not bother with trying truthfully to serve the Trinity. If your truth must be served up as first principles, foundational insights, or universally valid propositions, then you need not bother with the text that we call Scripture, which claims that all the truth we need has met us in a Jew from Nazareth.

Now the truth can be told. For us Christians, all truth *is* "relative," relative to this Jew named Jesus. We really do not know what the world is, much less where it is headed, until we know him. Jesus does not start with abstract propositions that are alleged to be univer-

---

11. See Alasdair C. MacIntyre, *After Virtue: A Study in Moral Theory*, 2d ed. (Notre Dame, Ind.: University of Notre Dame Press, 1984); and Cornel West, *Prophesy Deliverance! An Afro-American Revolutionary Christianity* (Philadelphia: Westminster, 1982).

sally valid, objectively true, or other such external prior conceptions of truth. Rather, he begins with the truth that is a person, personal, embodied, and enacted. "I am the way, and the truth, and the life," he says (John 14:6). *I* am truth. Therefore he is able to define what is true, not by arguing that certain aspects of the kingdom are congruent with what we think truth to be, but rather by parable, pronouncement, and enactment of that truth which is God's kingdom: "The kingdom of God is like...."

For us, Easter is not true because it "really happened" or is "historically true" or is "true to our experience of the presence of Christ," though it may indeed be all of that. We must not begin with our categories of what Easter would need to be if it were to be judged by us as true. Our lust for absolute, irrefutable truth is somehow tied to our modern attempt to define and, thereby, to harness and to wield absolute power. As Susan Bordo has shown, the Enlightenment arose, in great part, out of a profound anxiety about certitude. We wanted sure, self-derived, objective knowledge and devised an epistemology that would deliver it to us.[12] This was the counterpart of the Baconian attempt to understand in order to control. Yet Easter, by its very nature, is not something we can grasp or control (recall John 20:11–18, where the risen Christ frustrates Mary's attempt to "hold on to me"). The very diversity of the texts about Easter is testimony to disciples who had their categories and concepts, their very world, disrupted by resurrection. They struggle to bring to speech what their language was inept at describing. The creativity and intensity of their linguistic struggle are testimony to its credibility.

Easter is true because the text says it is true, because what the text says is true to the church's continuing engagement by the living Christ. It requires, not certitude, the sure fixing of truth, but rather trust, a playful willingness to let the strangeness of the text have its way with us.[13] The text has subsumed us into itself, rendered unto us a world that would have been unavailable to us without the world having been constructed (as most worlds are) by the text. Yet that does

---

12. Susan Bordo, *The Flight to Objectivity* (Albany: State University of New York Press, 1987). Especially, see Walter Brueggemann's explication of this theme in the first chapter of his *Texts under Negotiation: The Bible and Postmodern Imagination* (Minneapolis: Fortress, 1993).

13. See David J. Bryant, *Faith and the Play of Imagination: On the Role of Imagination in Religion* (Macon, Ga.: Mercer University Press, 1989).

not mean that the world rendered thereby exists only in the imagination of the text. Every time the church gathers, breaks the bread, and drinks the wine, we proclaim to any who dare to listen that what the text says, is. The text, we believe, has the power to evoke that which it describes.

We have the text, we believe, as a gracious gift of a God determined not to leave us to our own devices. What happened on Easter, namely, Jesus' coming back to us, refusing to leave us alone, intruding among us, is what happens each Sunday in the reading and preaching of the text. Scripture, read and preached, is Easter all over again. And, thank God, we never exhaust the significance of it, despite our most thorough interpretive efforts, for the text and the world it renders are thick. There is always a surplus of meaning, even after the longest of our sermons.

Thus John ends his account (at least *one* of his accounts) of Easter by preaching,

> Now Jesus did many other signs in the presence of his disciples, which are not written in this book. But these are written so that you may come to believe that Jesus is the Messiah, the Son of God, and that through believing you may have life in his name.
>
> (John 20:30–31)

11

PREACHING IN AN AGE THAT HAS LOST ITS MORAL COMPASS

William H. Willimon

"For the 1995 Easter issue of the *Journal for Preachers*, write an article on 'Preaching in a Culture That Has Lost Its Moral Compass.'" That was the article requested by the editors; this is the article they got.

This article was supposed to be a sort of Billy Graham tirade on how we ought to preach in an age that has lost its way, morally speaking. Begin with instances of the moral mess in America, Bill Bennett's tokens of a crumbling culture — declining SAT scores, pregnancies out of wedlock, deaths due to murder. Then move to the ways we preachers may prophetically address these ills in our sermons. That was the article I wanted to write; this is the article I wrote.

Something in us preachers would love to point to instances of ethical putrefaction in our congregations. When you stand up to preach on Sunday mornings, it's First Church Corinth all over again, maybe Sodom and Gomorrah, depending on your geographical location. How I love to fulminate against *their* sin! How we love to think of ethics as a series of detached ethical quandaries suffered by our parishioners.

Yet back in December, the second Sunday of Advent, a prickly text from Malachi jerked me by my clerical collar, shook me up and down, and spoke:

> But who can endure the day of his coming, and who can stand when he appears? For he is like a refiner's fire and like fullers' soap; ... and he will purify the descendants of Levi and refine them like gold and silver. (Mal. 3:2–3)

Don't worry, I assured my December congregation, the prophet is not talking about you. A wrath-filled God is coming to the temple, but not for you. God's after those who make their living at the temple, *the clergy:* "He will purify the descendants of Levi and refine them...until they present offerings to the LORD in righteousness" (3:3). We priests, contemporary "descendants of Levi," we who live off of religion, praying, prophesying, preaching, making offerings to God in behalf of the people, squirm when Malachi raves about the "priests, who despise my name. You say, 'How have we despised your name?'...By thinking that the LORD's table may be despised....I have no pleasure in you, says the LORD...I will not accept an offering from your hands" (1:6–7, 10).

God says to us clergy, "You wear me out" (1:13, author's paraphrase).

"The lips of a priest should guard knowledge, and people should seek instruction from his mouth, for he is the messenger of the LORD of hosts. But you have turned aside from the way; you have caused many to stumble by your instruction" (2:7–8), says Malachi. (Here, of course, the prophet is speaking of clergy who are also professors of theology in seminaries.)

After the prophet takes a swipe at priests who have committed adultery and fooled around with various members of the choir (2:14–16, you can look it up), then begins the Advent call from Malachi: "Who can endure the day of the LORD's coming? He is like a refiner's fire, like...soap...and he will purify the descendants of Levi" (Mal. 3:2 NRSV).[1]

Shortly after the night I was ordained, I read that pharmacists bested clergy in the annual list of the "most admired" professions. Then we were beat in the "most admired" list by firemen, letter carriers, and AMWAY distributors.

At the beginning of 1994, *The Christian Century* had a recap of the most significant religious news from the past year. One story was of a number of prominent priests charged with sexual abuse of children. Another told about a major embezzlement case at a large church in the Midwest. Malfeasance at the National Council of Churches.

---

1. See Elizabeth Achtemeier's commentary for a fine exposition of this passage in *Nahum–Malachi, Interpretation* (Louisville: Westminster/John Knox, 1986).

Clergy-laity trysts in Texas. We mainline clergy snickered when the news was of the sexual shenanigans of TV evangelists, but this was close to home, mainline liberals, and none of us laughed.

When a fellow United Methodist preacher from Fort Worth bit the dust this fall after his multiple sexual harassment episodes were made public by some courageous women, his fall hardly merited the headlines, for so many of his fellow clergy had fallen before him.

A friend of mine, an economist, was asked to serve on the board of a church charitable organization that helps needy children. His first days on the board were a sort of religious conversion experience for him, so inspired was he by the work of the organization, so impressed was he by the tremendous amount of need. But then he learned of the salaries, the real salaries, of some of the clergy staff. He uncovered accounting irregularities. After prayerful consideration, he brought it to the attention of the directors and...he was dismissed from the board.[2] He told me, "I think clergy, because they tell themselves that they are doing the work of the Lord, are particularly susceptible to self-deceit. If you're feeding hungry children, none of the moral rules apply to you which apply to other mere mortals."

Malachi, and the words of a Yahweh worn out by clergy, have summoned me to consider the loss of a moral compass, not among our congregations, but among us clergy. We preachers need look, alas, for signs of ethical disorientation, no farther than the pulpit.

Moral Confusion and Sin

My friend Stanley Hauerwas was recently asked about the moral confusion of contemporary clergy. Hauerwas said something to the effect that, "You have these people who get out of seminary thinking that their job is to 'help people.' That's where the adultery begins."

What?

"So you have these clergy," he continued, "who have no better reason for being in ministry than to 'meet peoples' needs.' So little Johnny needs picking up after school. And Johnny's mother, since she is working, calls the pastor, who has nothing else better to do, and

---

2. See Randy Frame, "Christian Children's Fund Practices Questioned," *Christianity Today* (November 14, 1994): 71.

asks him to pick up little Johnny. And the pastor thinks, 'Well, I'm here to help people.' So he goes and picks up little Johnny. Before long the pastor meets a parishioner who is lonely and needs love and then, when caught in the act of adultery, his defense is that he is an extremely caring pastor."[3]

I recalled what I thought to be, at the time, a rather silly article entitled "Clergy Adultery as Role Confusion" in *The Christian Century* by (who else?) a pastoral care professor. I wondered, "What about "Clergy Adultery as *Sin*"? But the more I have thought about it, the more I see that professor's point. In a culture of omnivorous need, all-consuming narcissism, clergy who have no more compelling motive for their preaching role than "meeting peoples' needs" are dangerous to themselves and to a culture without a moral compass.

Certainly, there are many possible sources of clerical moral ineptitude. Malachi would little understand the ways in which we clergy have been encouraged to wallow in the same psychotherapeutic mire as our people — meeting our needs; looking out for number one; if it feels good, do it; the relentless scanning and feeding of the ego. Yet Malachi would surely call us back (or is it *forward?*) to clerical lives grasped by something greater than ourselves, namely, our vocation to speak and to enact the Word of God among God's people. Here is my modest thesis: *We would be better people, you and I, if we were more faithful preachers.*

Clergy ethics has its basis in homiletics. Morality is a matter, not of being unattached to any external determination, free to think and act on the basis of our personal feelings of what's right. Contrary to the beliefs of liberalism, morality comes as a gracious by-product of being attached to something greater than ourselves, of being owned, claimed, commandeered for larger purposes,[4] which is to say that any account of the moral life begins and ends with the question, Who is the God whom we worship?

---

3. Hauerwas and I worked on some of these themes earlier in our article "The Limits of Care: Burnout as an Ecclesial Issue," *Word and World* (summer 1990): 247–53.

4. I am following an argument here similar to that of Stanley Hauerwas in his article "Practice Preaching" in the Advent 1994 issue of the *Journal for Preachers*, which is reprinted here in chapter 4. Indeed, you might want to go back and review that article, reading it in tandem with this one. You might also see my article "Why Being a Pastor Is More Important Than Being a 'Person,'" *Theology Today* 50 (1994): 580–85.

Letting the Word Speak

My own moral ineptitude, and its link with my homiletical deficiencies, was brought home to me a few years ago. Shortly after the Persian Gulf War, I received a note from one of the older members of my congregation, a note written on light blue stationery, neatly folded, a note written in a frail, but still lovely, hand.

"Have you preached on this particular episode, have you mentioned it in one of your recent sermons? Now that I can't get out and about, I listen on the radio to your sermons, but I do not recall your having mentioned this."

She was referring to a newspaper story (the clipping neatly folded within the same light blue envelope) about how American troops had buried alive as many as six hundred Iraqi soldiers in their trenches during a battle. "By the time we got there," one soldier was quoted as saying, "all that was left was hands and arms sticking up out of the sand."

"What does this do to the moral character of our nation?" she asked, in graceful, antique handwriting on the blue notepaper. "I grieve for the soul of our country. Where is the moral voice of our clergy in these matters?"

Her words stunned me into a renewal of my vocation. The problem, it seemed to me now, was not that I had been too timid in my preaching, too fixated in pop psychology to notice the ethical cataclysm taking place outside our sanctuary, too absorbed with the purely personal problems of my affluent congregation — although I am. My problem was not morality in itself. My problem was that I had not been enough of a preacher to let the Word have its way with me and my preaching. I have worshiped at the wrong altar.[5]

I recalled a wonderful comment by Walter Brueggemann, something said to us preachers like, "If you are a coward by nature, don't worry. You don't have to be courageous to be a preacher. All you have

---

5. This woman's exhortation to me, her preacher, illustrates Stanley Hauerwas's assertion in "Practice Preaching" that

preaching is not what a preacher does, but rather it is the activity of the whole community. Preaching as practice is the activity of the church that requires the church to be as able listeners, well-schooled and well-crafted hearers, as the preacher is the proclaimer. Indeed, I suspect one of the great difficulties of preaching in the church today is the preachers' presumption that those to whom they preach do not have ears well trained to

to do is to get down behind the text. You can say, 'This is not nec-
essarily me saying this — but I do think the text says it.'" We can
hunker down behind the text! Disjoined from service to the text, all I
can do is to serve the congregational status quo, run pastoral errands
for the world as it is, rather than let God use me to create a new
world. And that is not only no fun; it's also immoral.

I must make clear in my preaching that I preach what I have
been *told* to preach.[6] I serve the text, not those who listen. I must
thereby help my listeners recover the adventure of being those who
are baptized to listen to the text, those who bear the burden and the
blessing of bending our lives in conformity to the demands of Scripture.[7] Morality is always a liturgical matter; who is the god whom we
worship?

In a culture that has lost its moral compass (what we did in Iraq
for Exxon has its counterpart in what we are doing to one another in
bedrooms), that old lady's note on blue stationery called me back to
the ethical significance of preaching.

Serving a True Master or a False One

I would like every seminarian in my denomination to read what is,
in my opinion, one of the best novels of the late nineteenth century,
certainly one of the best novels on the peculiar moral dilemmas of
clergy. It is Harold Frederic's *The Damnation of Theron Ware* (1896).
A young Methodist preacher is called to preach, but called more so to
advance socially through his preaching. Stifled by the confines of petty
morality in the midwestern town where he serves, Mr. Ware longs for
a larger stage on which to display his homiletical talents. His best
friends — the urbane Father Forbes of the nearby Catholic church;

---

hear. As a result, preaching is not the practice of the community but rather, as it so often
is, an exercise in sentimentality (see p. 64 of this volume).

It should be noted that this woman was an eighty-year-old Presbyterian. She had been
trained, I presume, to expect something of her preachers and to hold her preacher accountable
through her own "preaching" on the light blue notepaper.

6. Again, Hauerwas in "Practice Preaching": "For preaching to be a practice intrinsic to
the worship of God requires that the preacher, as well as the congregation, stand under the
authority of the Word. That is why preaching should rightly follow a lectionary . . . the exercise
of the ministry of proclamation requires ministers to make clear that the Word preached is as
painful to them as it is to the congregation" (see p. 64 of this volume).

7. See my *Peculiar Speech: Preaching to the Baptized* (Grand Rapids: Eerdmans, 1992).

Dr. Ledsmar, the town's one social Darwinian; and Celia Madden, a wealthy connoisseur of the arts — represent all that Ware wants to be in life. The more these friends urge him to sample a social life out of his present reach, the less he regards his own ministerial vocation. His vocation becomes a career, a path up the social ladder through the flattering, eloquent art of his preaching.

Adultery (what is there about us clergy that makes us so susceptible to this temptation?)[8] is not far behind. When Ware finally confesses his love for Celia, she announces to him that his presumed "improvement" has only served to render a once adequate pastor into a first-class bore. Ware eventually leaves the ministry, victim of his own craving for status and recognition.[9]

Of course, Ware's descent to the level of a rather common adulterer has nothing to do with his inability to meet his personal needs or with his being out of touch with his feelings as a man. His descent is related to his inability to be attached to his vocation as a preacher. When that vocation becomes a mere means to an end, flaws in the preacher's character, which may have been overcome by the preacher's commitment to the ethics of good preaching, are magnified.

Elsewhere I have reflected upon the great fiction of our age, the notion of the person without a role, the idea that we are most fully moral when we have divested ourselves of all external claims upon us.[10] The liberal self, detached from any history, any claim upon the self other than the claims one has personally chosen, does not exist. All of us are busy being determined by something — even the claim

---

8. The modern poet C. H. Sisson in a mock address to John Donne, the preacher, notes a curious relationship between preaching, sex, and ambition:

> "...the vain, the ambitious and the highly sexed
> Are the natural prey of the Incarnate Christ."

See C. H. Sisson, "A Letter to John Donne," in *New Oxford Book of Christian Verse* (Oxford University Press, 1981), 285.

9. For more recent fictional treatments of the moral demise of preachers, see James P. Wind, "Clergy Ethics in Modern Fiction," in *Clergy Ethics in a Changing Society: Mapping the Terrain,* ed. J. P. Wind, R. Burck, P. F. Camenisch, and D. P. McCann (Louisville: Westminster/John Knox, 1991), 180–87.

I would add the following to my list of required moral reading for clergy: Peter DeVries, *The Mackeral Plaza,* 1958; Nathaniel Hawthorne, *The Scarlet Letter;* John Updike, *A Month of Sundays,* 1974; and Andrew Greeley, *Thy Brother's Wife,* 1982.

10. William H. Willimon, "Clergy Ethics: Getting Our Story Straight," in *Against the Grain: New Approaches to Professional Ethics,* ed. Michael Goldberg (Valley Forge, Pa.: Trinity, 1993), 60–69.

that I am living only "for myself" is an externally imposed claim by contemporary American society. So the question is not, Will I serve some purpose larger than myself?[11] for freedom from such determination is impossible. The question is, Will the master whom I serve be true or false?[12]

Preachers are those who are fortunate enough to have our lives caught up in the demanding, never quite finished, wonderful adventure of helping the church to hear God's Word. Aristotle taught that it was too much to expect ordinary people to be good. About the best one could do for ordinary folk was to teach them good habits. Of the three artistic forms of proof that Aristotle listed as available to the public speaker — logos, pathos, and ethos — Aristotle knew that ethos, the character of the speaker, "constitutes the most effective means of proof" (*Rhetoric* 1.2).[13] Every time we stand up to preach, our characters, as they have been formed by the habits required for preaching, prove to the church that it is possible to make very ordinary folk (like preachers) into saints. That is, it is possible even for people who are innate liars to speak the truth. It is possible for people who are cowards by nature to be so caught up in some project greater than themselves that, despite themselves, they are heroic. I think it was after tackling a particularly difficult preaching assignment that Paul was bold enough to say to the Philippians, "Brothers and sisters, join in imitating me..." (Phil. 3:17a NRSV).

Homiletical habits — disciplined, weekly study; honesty and humility about what the text says and does not say; confidence in the ability of God to make our puny congregations worthy to hear God's Word; a weekly willingness to allow the Word to devastate the preacher before it lays a hand on the congregation — all these are habits, skills of the homiletical craft, that form us preachers into bet-

---

11. "This is the true joy in life, the being used for a purpose recognized by yourself as a mighty one;...the being a force of Nature instead of a feverish selfish little clod of ailments and grievances complaining that the world will not devote itself to making you happy." George Bernard Shaw, epistle dedicatory to *Man and Superman* (Westminster: Archibald Constavle & Co., Ltd., 1903)]

12. This point is argued so well in Stanley Fish's reply to Stephen Carter, "Liberalism Doesn't Exist," *The Duke Law Journal* (1987): 997.

13. Richard Lischer, *Theories of Preaching* (Durham, N.C.: Labyrinth, 1987), 3, notes how the great homiletical treatises after Augustine and through the Middle Ages, as well as the later work of homileticians like Baxter and Schleiermacher, expend much energy in discussions of the character of the preacher.

ter people than we would be if we had been left to our own devices. I think this is what Paul was getting at when he told the Corinthians that it would have been nice if he could have preached to them with flattering, eloquent words, but being a preacher, he single-mindedly "decided to know nothing among you except Jesus Christ, and him crucified" (1 Cor. 2:2).

Yes, we live in a culture that has lost its moral compass. Lies are told on the floor of the Senate and in bedrooms. We pass by the "hands and arms sticking up out of the sand" without a twitch of conscience. In such a time, it is easy to lose our way. Therefore we preachers would do well to cling to our vocation, to determine to know nothing save that which the church has called us to preach, to serve the Word before we bow before other gods.

That dear, departed resident alien among us, William Stringfellow, said it so much more eloquently than I, with his words, with his life:

> To know the Word of God in the Bible, a person must come to the Bible with a certain naivety, confessing that if God exists at all, God lives independently, though not in isolation, from anyone's intelligence, longing, emotion, insight, or interpretations, even those that divine the truth. One must be open to God's initiative, be bereft of all preconceptions, surrender all initiative.... One must take the appalling risk.... When a person is so naked, so helpless, so transparent, when one so utterly ceases to try to justify oneself or anyone or anything else, one first becomes vulnerable to the Word of God.... When a person becomes that mature as a human being, he or she is freed to listen and at last to welcome the Word.... That person is enlightened to discern the same Word of God at work now in the world.... Thus is established a rhythm in the Christian's life encompassing intimacy with the Word of God in the Bible and one's involvement with the same Word active in the world.[14]

Who could blame the great God for being worn out with us clergy (Mal. 1:13)? Our poor preaching, Malachi indicates, is not just a mat-

---

14. William Stringfellow, *Count It All Joy: Reflections on Faith, Doubt, and Temptation* (Grand Rapids: Eerdmans, 1967), 20. Bill Wylie Kellermann has edited a wonderful volume of William Stringfellow's writings, which is aptly titled *A Keeper of the Word* (Grand Rapids: Eerdmans, 1994).

ter of lousy homiletical technique;[15] it is also a failure of character, a moral matter of tragic proportions. Yet this is the season of resurrection. For us preachers the Easter prophetic promise is that the Lord may even yet purify us descendants of Levi, may soap us down, fire us up, call us back to our chief task — to be yoked so securely and joyously to the Word that in the process of proclamation of the Word, we become the Word as it dwells in us richly.

---

15. Stanley Hauerwas has suggested that ethical theory was devised as an attempt to have ethics without character. Through rules and principles we hope to achieve the good deeds that come, not from right rules and principles, but from good people. There is a sense in which I believe that homiletical theory and technique may be an attempt to have good preaching without having preachers with the requisite character for good preaching.

See also Stanley M. Hauerwas, "Clerical Character," in *Christian Existence Today* (Durham, N.C.: Labyrinth, 1988), 133–48.

12

EASTER PREACHING AS PECULIAR SPEECH

William H. Willimon

When I emerged from seminary and began to preach, I thought that about the worst fate that could befall me as a preacher was not to be heard. It was my task, through the homiletical, rhetorical arts, to bridge the gap, the great communicative gap, between speaker and listener. I now know that I had been taught to misconstrue the gap. The gap, the evangelical distance that ought to concern the preacher, is not one of time — the time between Jesus and us — nor is it one of communication — the space between speaker and listener. The gap that is the main concern of the evangelical preacher is the space between us and the gospel. Contemporary homiletical thought has focused upon style, rhetoric, or method when theology ought to be our concern. Our problem as preachers is not that we must render strange biblical stories intelligible to modern people but rather that these biblical stories render a strange God.

There are many reasons why we fail to communicate as preachers that have to do with our limitations as preachers. We don't communicate because we lack certain homiletical skills, because we don't prepare, because we don't know enough about the gospel; we misunderstand the human condition. But there are also many excellent reasons for our failure to communicate.

In sermon preparation, I quickly learned that some of my most unfaithful preaching arose in that moment when, after having studied the biblical text, I asked myself, "So what?" That's where the trouble

Portions of this article are adapted from my *The Intrusive Word: Preaching to the Unbaptized* (Grand Rapids: Eerdmans, 1994).

starts — in my homiletical attempt to answer the "So what?" question. Trouble is, I will invariably misconstrue the communicative gap between my people and the gospel. My answer to the "So what?" question will be limited by my present horizons, by conventional ideas of what can and cannot be. Evangelism, unlike apologetics, seeks transformation on the part of speaker and hearer.[1] Evangelism expects, promises, transformation. Refusing to traffic in the conventional epistemologies of the present age and its beneficiaries, evangelism says that we will never know anything worth knowing without conversion:

> ...put away your former way of life, your old self, corrupt and deluded by its lusts, and...be renewed in the spirit of your minds, and...clothe yourselves with the new self, created according to the likeness of God in true righteousness and holiness. (Eph. 4:22–24)

The images of stripping off clothes and throwing away our past are surely baptismal. Everything starts and ends with baptism. If our speech doesn't move uninformed people outside the church toward baptism, or at least move jaded, tired, unformed people inside the church to a renewal of their baptism, our talk is not evangelical. Apologetics is what we do when we don't want to risk being transformed. Apologetics is Campus Crusade's Josh McDowell coming to campus to talk about sex, then, in the last five minutes of his speech, dangling out Jesus as the answer to everything that ails us, including our sick sex. All that proves is that sex is more important than Jesus. We start with sex, bowing to its dominance in our lives, and then, after having established an intellectual community on that basis, slyly move our hearers to think about Jesus. Apologetics gives up too much intellectual territory before the battle begins seeking mere agreement rather than transformation, intellectual detoxification.

This is my major disagreement with Leander Keck's *The Church Confident.*[2] Realizing that mainline Protestant Christianity is in big

---

1. See Stanley Hauerwas's criticism of apologetics in William H. Willimon and Stanley M. Hauerwas, *Preaching to Strangers: Evangelism in Today's World* (Louisville: Westminster/John Knox, 1992), 1–15.

2. Leander E. Keck, *The Church Confident* (Nashville: Abingdon, 1993). Keck dismisses my book (with Stanley Hauerwas) *Resident Aliens* as "inappropriate for the mainline churches" (76). Here I continue to bet that Keck is wrong in his belief that the mainline churches are "tone

trouble, Keck calls upon us Protestant preachers to be more confident about what we have to say; to assert, ever more skillfully and confidently, fairly much what we have said before. Keck's is a justification, albeit a very skillfully done justification, for business as usual in the American church. The faith that he would have us assert more confidently is the pre-1940s faith that Americans (if church numbers are to be believed) appear to have relinquished. The mainline Protestantism that Keck defends fared quite well during times of American cultural confidence; after all, it was the faith engendered by that culture, the faith of mainline Protestant liberalism, that so hoped to be of service to the culture. However, as the '70s began and increasing numbers of Americans realized that something was wrong in their nation, in their marriages and families, the self-confident liberalism of the mainliners wilted, and people either deserted us in droves or greeted us with a yawn. As the culture disintegrated, a church that found its main justification for existence in keeping that culture afloat seemed pointless.

Besides, there are excellent reasons why we don't communicate. People bring many things with them in their listening to a sermon. Having been preconditioned, their ears are not in tune with the message; their understanding is blocked by metaphors that enable them to participate in the culture but that make it difficult for them to hear the gospel. We evangelists ought to throw the mantle of forgiveness over some of our homiletical failures. Desiring too desperately to communicate, at any cost, can lead us into apostasy. The odd way in which God has saved us presents a never-ending challenge to those who are called to talk about it.

Recently, a woman who was a practitioner of something she called "destructivist art" spoke to my freshman seminar. Destructivist art involves, at least in her case, throwing hydrochloric acid on a canvas, while viewers watch the canvas rot due to the eating away of the canvas by the acid. This is alleged to be some sort of statement about our cultural situation.

After she showed the class examples of her art, some of the class

---

deaf to such a summons" (75). In this respect, I am more confident about mainline American Protestantism than Keck. I really do believe that we are capable of being so faithful (rather than so confident in the theology and style of our recent past) that Americans might again find us to be interesting.

said, "This is the most wonderful thing I've ever seen." However, the majority of the class felt totally excluded by her communication. Many of them were angry. "This is not art!" they blurted out. "This is demeaning to the whole notion of art. If this is art, anybody can do it."

She responded, "Anyone could do it, but the important thing is that *I* did it. The other important thing is that you don't know what I am doing." She responded to their questions with grace and good humor. However, by the end of the class, most of the students were still unconvinced, uncomprehending, of her work.

What impressed me as a Christian communicator was her absolute willingness to have them not understand her. She was utterly willing for them to walk out of the class, as befuddled by her art at the end of the class as they were when the class began.

"There are good reasons for not understanding this art. Don't be so hard on yourself," she reassured them. "This art is very demanding on the viewer. If I am really making a critique of the present structures of society, then if one is caught in one of those structures, or benefiting from those structures, there are good reasons why one should not be able to understand this art. In a way, your inability to comprehend this art is, in itself, a validation of what I'm claiming to be the aims of this art."

Can we preachers respect the gospel enough to allow people not to understand it? We are not responsible for all failures of communication. The gospel itself, in collision with the corruptions engendered by life in a democratic, capitalist society, bears some of the responsibility for people not hearing. We preachers so want to be heard that we are willing to make the gospel more accessible than it really is, to remove the scandal, the offense of the cross, to deceive people into thinking that it is possible to hear without conversion. This is the great lie behind most of my apologetics, the deceit behind the current enthusiasm for "inductive" preaching — that it is possible to hear the gospel while we are still trapped in outmoded, culturally conditioned patterns of thought and hearing. How are we extricated from such patterns? How does the gospel manage to work such power among epistemologically enslaved folk like us?

I don't know. It's a miracle.

The Listener as King

In this respect we are heirs of Charles G. Finney, a lawyer called by God from his law practice in 1821 by "a retainer from the Lord Jesus Christ to plead his cause." Finney invented the "protracted meeting" for revivals, introduced the "anxious bench" for sinners, and developed the team approach to planning for a revival. "Revival is not a miracle, or dependent on a miracle in any sense. It is a purely philosophical [i.e., scientific] result of the right use of the constituted means," said Finney in his 1835 *Lectures on Revivalism*. Today, we have forgotten that there was once a time when preachers had to defend their preoccupation with listener response to their Calvinist detractors, who thought that the gospel was more important than its listeners.

I am here arguing that revivals *are* miraculous, that the gospel is so odd, so against the grain of our natural inclinations and the infatuations of our culture, that nothing less than a miracle is required in order for there to be true hearing. My position is therefore closer to that of the Calvinist Jonathan Edwards than to Finney. Edwards labored as pastor in Northampton, Massachusetts, for an uneventful seven lean years until his congregation experienced a series of what Edwards called "surprising conversions." Edwards, who is one of the greatest minds America has produced, was wonderfully befuddled by this outbreak of religious vitality. In 1737 he wrote an account of the affair, delightfully called *A Faithful Narrative of the Surprising Work of God in the Conversion of Many Hundred Souls in Northampton, and Neighboring Towns and Villages*. I like to think that Edwards was such a great mind, had such an understanding of the peculiarity of the gospel, coupled with an awareness of the cognitive intransigence of his people, that he was therefore genuinely surprised when anyone heard, really heard, and responded to his preaching. We ought also to be surprised.

The homiletical future, alas, lay with Finney rather than Edwards. The logical culmination of Finney's theological weaknesses, the "new measures" for our day, are to be found not only in the inductive-preaching proponents, who measure all preaching on the basis of listener response, but also in the new genre of church-marketing books typified by the work of George Barna, church-growth strategist. In popular books for clergy with names like *Marketing the Church* and *User Friendly Churches,* Barna tells us that,

> Jesus Christ was a communications specialist. He communicated His message in diverse ways, and with results that would be a credit to modern advertising and marketing agencies. Notice the Lord's approach: He identified His target audience, determined their need, and delivered His message directly. . . . He promoted His product in the most efficient way possible: by communicating with the "hot prospects."
>
> Don't underestimate the marketing lessons Jesus taught. He understood His product thoroughly, developed an unparalleled distribution system, advanced a method of promotion that has penetrated every continent, and offered His product at a price that is within the grasp of every consumer (without making the product so accessible that it lost its value).[3]

In *Resident Aliens: Life in the Christian Colony,* Stanley Hauerwas and I suggested that there was much atheism lurking behind some of our preaching, pastoral care, and church administration. Atheism is the conviction that the presence and power of God are unessential to the work of ministry, that we can find the right technique, the proper approach, the appropriate attitude, and therefore will not need God to validate our ministry. If Jesus was the "communications specialist"

---

3. George Barna, *Marketing the Church: What They Never Taught You about Church Growth* (Colorado Springs, Colo.: NavPress, 1988), 50. For an extensive, evangelical critique of Barna and the entire church marketing movement, see Douglas D. Webster, *Selling Jesus* (Downers Grove, Ill.: InterVarsity, 1992). Walter Brueggemann's corrective on Barna's type of "church growth" is helpful here:

> . . . evangelism is related *to church growth,* related but in no way synonymous. In speaking of evangelism, one must speak of church growth, but only at the end of the dramatic process, and not any sooner. Evangelism is never aimed at institutional enhancement or aggrandizement. It is aimed simply and solely at summoning people to new, liberated obedience to the true governor of all created reality. The church is a modest gathering locus for those serious about the new governance. There must be such a gathering . . . because the new governance is inherently against autonomy, isolation, and individualism. The church grows because more and more persons change allegiance, switch worlds, accept the new governance and agree to the unending and difficult task of appropriating the news in practical ways. "Church growth" misserves evangelism, however, when the church is allied with consumerism, for then the church talks people out of the very obedience to which the news summons us.

See Walter Brueggemann, *Biblical Perspectives on Evangelism: Living in a Three-Storied Universe* (Nashville: Abingdon, 1993), 45.

that Barna claims him to be, why in the world did he waste so much time teaching "in parables" that few understood? Above all, if he was so good at communication, why on earth was he crucified?

We must learn to preach again in such a way as to demonstrate that if Jesus has not been raised from the dead, then our preaching is doomed to fall upon deaf ears. Our preaching ought to be so confrontative, so in violation of all that contemporary Americans think they know, that it requires no less than a miracle to be heard. We preach best with a reckless confidence in the power of the gospel to evoke the audience it deserves.

I find myself agreeing with Robin R. Meyers when he says, "Preachers are too eager to make sure that everyone understands, that everyone gets it. This inevitably means that too much of the obvious is explained, and too little of the mysterious is described." Yet I part company with Meyers when he contends, "We are not using symbolic language to achieve some sort of conceptual precision, rather we are using metaphors to generate the insight that comes from recognizing common human experience."[4] "Common human experience" doesn't exist, and even if it did, it should not be confused with the gospel. There are only different stories, which evoke and engender various kinds of human experiences. The gospel is one of them, a story that we believe to be not only mysterious and interesting but also *true*. Church is the human experience evoked by the gospel. Preaching is not a means to evoke certain "common human experience" through the artful use of metaphor and simile. Preaching means to engender experience we would never have had without the gospel.

In Meyers's book, *With Ears to Hear*, he speaks about preaching as if our challenge were mainly a problem of our inadequate use of rhetoric, a problem of style, delivery, method. His book is rather typical of the tendency within modern homiletics to fixate on com-

---

4. Robin R. Meyers, *With Ears to Hear: Preaching as Self-Persuasion* (Cleveland: Pilgrim, 1993), 79. The problem with Meyers's book is, not simply its overreliance on Fred B. Craddock's *As One without Authority*, but its rather shocking thesis that "Self-persuasion theory rests on one very simple but central premise: the messages we generate for ourselves are more authoritative than those from an outside source. This clear and decisive break with classical rhetoric locates persuasion at the ear of the listener, not at the mouth of the rhetor. And there exists a substantial body of research to back up the claim that when it comes to authority, the holiest of trinities is Me, Myself, and I" (49). As a wonderful statement of the uphill battle to be waged each Sunday by the evangelical preacher, I can do no better than this. As a basis for homiletical theory, such a thesis must be rejected on the basis of the peculiarity of trinitarian faith.

municative method rather than theological substance, a tendency that I pilloried in *Peculiar Speech*. [5] There is certainly much to be learned by preachers about rhetoric and method, and Meyers's book is helpful. However, I am arguing that failure to hear is also based upon the nature of the gospel. Easter, as a divine assault upon human thought dominated by death, provokes misunderstanding. When Kierkegaard observed in *Either/Or* that "Truth is not nimble on its feet...it is not its own evangelist," perhaps he was indicating how large a task we have in communicating the gospel in a culture of lies. The gospel itself shares some of the "blame" for our communicative failures, contending, as the gospel does, that the solution to what ails us lies somewhere out beyond our selves.

G. K. Chesterton once said that if one is trying to communicate something to another person and the person says, "I don't understand," you will reach for some metaphor. You will say, "Well, it's like...." Then, if the person still responds, "I don't understand," you will try another metaphor. If the person still does not understand, then you must say, "You don't understand."[6]

More than that, I am arguing that bad preaching, as Meyers describes it, preaching so anxious that "everyone gets it," that it ends up expecting too much and saying too little, is often a factor of bad theology. We have so little trust in the power of the gospel to evoke the listeners the gospel deserves that we either simplify, simplify, reducing the gospel to a slogan for a bumper sticker, or else we poetically describe, describe, obfuscating the gospel with some allegedly "common human experience" that is unworthy of Easter. People live in the grip of stories that are not the gospel, stories that cannot generate the life for which they deeply yearn. Therefore I agree with Walter Brueggemann when he says that "evangelism means inviting people into these stories [the gospel] as the definitional story of our life, and thereby authorizing people to give up, abandon, and renounce other stories that have shaped their lives in false or distorting ways."[7]

---

5. *Peculiar Speech* (Grand Rapids: Eerdmans, 1992), 49–53.
6. G. K. Chesterton, *Orthodoxy* (New York: Doubleday, 1959), 78.
7. Brueggemann, *Biblical Perspectives on Evangelism, 10.*

Easter as the Basis for Christian Preaching

The gospel is an intrusion among us, not something arising out of us. Easter is the ultimate intrusion of God. The gap between our alliances with death and the God of life as revealed on Easter is the ultimate gap with which gospel preaching must contend. The muddle of different ways of describing what happened at Easter within the Gospels and Epistles themselves is testimony to the cognitive dissonance created by a God who came back. Early Christians preachers groped for some language adequate to the task of telling what happened on Easter.

Easter is the embarrassment the church can't get around. Yet in this embarrassment is the engine of our preaching. It is only because Jesus has been raised from the dead that I have confidence in preaching. It is only on the basis of the risen Christ's return to his disheartened followers after Easter that I presume that he has made me an agent of gospel subversion through preaching. If God did not triumph over Caesar and all the legions of death on Easter, then God will never triumph on Sunday in my church over *The Wall Street Journal* and Leo Buscaglia.

I don't preach Jesus' story in the light of my experience as some sort of helpful symbol or myth that is helpfully illumined by my story.[8] Rather, I am invited by Easter to interpret my story in the light of God's triumph in the resurrection. Only because we worship a resurrected Lord can we risk preaching. Our claims for preaching have little to do with a savvy utilization of various contemporary rhetorical insights; rather our claims arise from our very peculiar convictions about a very particular God. The essential patience required of preachers, freedom from homiletical anxiety over the reaction of our listeners, is possible only if in fact Jesus did rise from the tomb.

As Rowan Williams says,

> ...the Christian proclamation of the resurrection of the crucified just man, his return to his unfaithful friends and his empowering of them to forgive in his name offers a paradigm of

---

8. I fear this is what David Buttrick comes close to in his description of preaching Mark 16:1–8 as "symbol." See *Homiletic* (Philadelphia: Fortress, 1987), 399–404. Yet Buttrick's discussion of the resurrection and preaching on pp. 450–51 of his *Homiletic* certainly seems to confirm what I am claiming about preaching's linkage to Easter.

the "saving" process; yet not only a paradigm. It is a story which is itself an indispensable agent in the completion of this process, because it witnesses to the one personal agent in whose presence we may have full courage to "own" ourselves as sinners and full hope for a humanity whose identity is grounded in a recognition and affirmation by nothing less than God. It is a story which makes possible the comprehensive act of *trust*. [9]

I wish that I might preach in such a way as to require a miracle, a resurrection, in order to be heard. I wish that I might preach in such a way as to demonstrate my outrageous trust in the continuing reality of Easter, my utter dependence on God's inclination to work the unexpected. So many of the Easter narratives end with the command to "Go, tell." We may go and tell, not only because we now have, after Easter, some news to tell, namely, that Jesus shall reign, but also because, after Easter, we have the means to tell principally because the risen Christ continues to work life out of death in us wherever this story is faithfully told.

---

9. Rowan Williams, *Resurrection* (London: Darton, Longman & Todd, 1982), 49.

CONTRIBUTORS

ERSKINE CLARKE is editor and publisher of *Journal for Preachers,* and Professor of American Religious History, Columbia Theological Seminary, Decatur, Georgia.

WALTER BRUEGGEMANN is William Marcellus McPheeters Professor of Old Testament, Columbia Theological Seminary, Decatur, Georgia. He is an editor of *Journal for Preachers.*

STANLEY M. HAUERWAS is Gilbert T. Rowe Professor of Theological Ethics, The Divinity School, Duke University, Durham, North Carolina.

BARBARA BROWN TAYLOR is an Episcopal priest in the diocese of Atlanta and Harry R. Butman Professor of Religion and Philosophy, Piedmont College, Demorest, Georgia.

WILLIAM H. WILLIMON is Dean of the Chapel and Professor of Christian Ministry, The Divinity School, Duke University, Durham, North Carolina.